"PN Balji is a rare and wonderful fixture in that peculiar world known as journalism in Singapore. For almost four decades … Balji navigated a world where 'truth' was often a state-sanctioned commodity and real journalism was a perilous undertaking … Balji's insights into what it was like to practise journalism with integrity under these circumstances is an important contribution to the history of modern Singapore."

David Plott
former editor of the *Far Eastern Economic Review*
and managing editor of *Global Asia* (www.globalasia.org)

"Balji would loathe to admit it but he has raised a generation of intrepid journalists. A newsman ahead of his time, Balji's book contains not only fascinating behind-the-scenes accounts told in his trademark punchy style, it also holds deep lessons for tomorrow's journalists."

Loh Chee Kong
Deputy Chief Editor of *TODAY*

RELUCTANT EDITOR

THE SINGAPORE MEDIA AS SEEN THROUGH THE EYES OF A VETERAN NEWSPAPER JOURNALIST

PN BALJI

Marshall Cavendish Editions

© 2019 Marshall Cavendish International (Asia) Private Limited
Text © PN Balji

Published by Marshall Cavendish Editions
An imprint of Marshall Cavendish International

All rights reserved

No part of this publication may be reproduced, stored in a retrieval system or transmitted, in any form or by any means, electronic, mechanical, photocopying, recording or otherwise, without the prior permission of the copyright owner. Requests for permission should be addressed to the Publisher, Marshall Cavendish International (Asia) Private Limited, 1 New Industrial Road, Singapore 536196. Tel: (65) 6213 9300. E-mail: genref@sg.marshallcavendish.com
Website: www.marshallcavendish.com/genref

The publisher makes no representation or warranties with respect to the contents of this book, and specifically disclaims any implied warranties or merchantability or fitness for any particular purpose, and shall in no event be liable for any loss of profit or any other commercial damage, including but not limited to special, incidental, consequential, or other damages.

Other Marshall Cavendish Offices
Marshall Cavendish Corporation, 99 White Plains Road, Tarrytown NY 10591-9001, USA • Marshall Cavendish International (Thailand) Co Ltd, 253 Asoke, 12th Flr, Sukhumvit 21 Road, Klongtoey Nua, Wattana, Bangkok 10110, Thailand • Marshall Cavendish (Malaysia) Sdn Bhd, Times Subang, Lot 46, Subang Hi-Tech Industrial Park, Batu Tiga, 40000 Shah Alam, Selangor Darul Ehsan, Malaysia.

Marshall Cavendish is a registered trademark of Times Publishing Limited

National Library Board, Singapore Cataloguing in Publication Data

Names: P. N., Balji.
Title: Reluctant editor : the Singapore media as seen through the eyes of a veteran newspaper journalist / P N Balji.
Description: Singapore : Marshall Cavendish Editions, [2019]
Identifiers: OCN 1098016628 | ISBN 978-981-48-2820-8 (paperback)
Subjects: Journalism--Singapore. | Journalists--Singapore. | Reporters and reporting--Singapore.
Classification: DDC 079.5957--dc23

Printed in Singapore

CONTENTS

Foreword   7

Author's Note   9

Chapter 1   **My Father's Son**
The chapter I didn't want to write   15

Chapter 2   **Accidental Sub-editor, Reluctant Editor**
In a world of tabloids   23

Chapter 3   **Living Dangerously**
Who is that practising western-style journalism?   37

Chapter 4   **The Misunderstood Paper**
What a foreign editor saw that others did not   65

Chapter 5   **Toh Chin Chye Affair**
A footloose newsroom culture gone wrong   79

Chapter 6   **Indian Fever**
And TNP's role in it   91

Chapter 7   **Big, Bold and Sometimes Ugly**
An apology is in store   101

Chapter 8   **TODAY Bets on Goh Chok Tong**
Chairman Cheng makes split-second decision   111

Chapter 9   **TODAY Arrives, SPH Miscalculates**
And media history is made   121

Chapter 10   **Last of the Mohicans**
Why the editors of old did it differently   135

Annex   153

About the Author   196

FOREWORD

I thank my friend, PN Balji, for requesting me to write the Foreword for his memoirs. He is one of Singapore's veteran newspaper journalists and editors, and a very good one.

Balji worked with *The Straits Times*, *The New Paper*, *TODAY*, *Malay Mail* and *New Nation*. I think his greatest achievement as a journalist was during the ten-year period when he was the editor of the tabloid, *The New Paper*. He made the paper commercially successful and intellectually credible. He also did an unusually good job as editor of *TODAY*, in the face of fierce opposition.

Most intellectuals look down on the tabloids. I used to have the same attitude until I met a veteran journalist and good friend of Singapore, Arnold Brackman. He was a seasoned foreign correspondent, an expert on Indonesia and a good friend of Mr S Rajaratnam, our first Foreign Minister. He was teaching journalism at a college in Connecticut. One day, he asked me which newspapers I read every day. I said I read *The New York Times*, the *Wall Street Journal* and the *Washington Post*. Professor

Brackman advised me to subscribe to a New York tabloid. He reasoned that the three papers I read represented the elite opinions of America but not the opinions of the man in the street. I took his advice and started to read the *New York Post*, in addition to the three elite newspapers. The lesson I learnt from Brackman is that it is important to be in touch with the ground.

Coming back to *The New Paper*, I recall that the paper once asked me to write an article for them on ASEAN. I accepted the challenge. I wrote the article in very simple English and free of jargon. I submitted my article and received quite a shock when the editor of the paper told me that his readers wouldn't understand my article. The editor rewrote my article in a language and style which was more accessible to his readers. It was a humbling experience. It taught me that writing for *The New Paper* was an art which I did not possess.

I have always admired our journalists. They work under many constraints. My friend, Cheong Yip Seng's book, *OB Markers: My Straits Times Story*, gives a detailed account of the kinds of pressure under which they work. I particularly admire the journalists who have not caved in to the pressure but are able to maintain their integrity. Singapore needs a press which is both independent and responsible.

Tommy Koh
Professor of Law
National University of Singapore

AUTHOR'S NOTE

Reluctant Editor is NOT a memoir and doesn't pretend to be one. It takes the reader through the five newspapers where I worked and highlights the challenges and successes I experienced, especially in the last two. I started my career at the *Malay Mail* in 1970 and progressed through *New Nation*, *The Straits Times*, *The New Paper* and *TODAY*.

The New Paper became my university of life, forcing my introverted self to break out of the cocoon to take risks that have the ability, even years later, to make me shudder each time I think about them. *TODAY* was an insurgent that dared to steal a crumb of *The Straits Times*' lunch. It compelled me to roll up my sleeves and, audaciously perhaps, take on the might of the print giant. Both papers broke new ground in Singapore media history: *The New Paper* as the only afternoon newspaper ever to top 50,000 in daily sales; and *TODAY* for unlocking *The Straits Times*' stranglehold on the morning newspaper market.

The other theme that runs through the book is how a group of editors, suckered by the rambunctious Fleet Street culture of England's newspapers, stood their ground when their principles would not let them give in to everything that Lee Kuan Yew wanted. One should not forget that Singapore's founding prime minister was at his rogue best at that time. How and why did they do things differently? I try to answer that question in the final chapter, "Last of the Mohicans".

There are NO photographs in this book. Sourcing for them would be a difficult task, as I realised when sounding out my former colleagues. Hardly anyone kept relevant photographs. I decided not to approach Singapore Press Holdings and Mediacorp as I felt there might be more to-ing and fro-ing than I cared for, and the cost would likely be prohibitive. Deep into my retirement, this was the last thing I wanted.

Reluctant Editor is NOT a comprehensive study of the Singapore media. This is a story, some aspects of which I was involved in. And in others I was a front-row witness.

I have organised *Reluctant Editor* thematically, NOT chronologically. This is deliberate as I felt that most readers will not have the time to plough through the important highs and lows and fit them into the two themes mentioned earlier. I sought to keep each chapter to about 4,000 words. Sometimes I got carried away and a few chapters busted the word count. My favourite chapters are "Toh Chin Chye Affair" and "Last of the Mohicans".

The saddest point in my career was to see a crisis envelope *The New Paper* newsroom, leading to a great reporter being told to leave and two smart editors being demoted. It was the most horrible sin to happen in a newspaper. It took us a while to recover and get back on our feet. Years later, as I recollect the sad episode, I do it with some pride. The reporter has gone on to become a significant member in the commodities industry while the two editors have shown great resilience to move on to important jobs in Singapore Press Holdings. This episode is related in Chapter 5.

I write about the three print giants of modern Singapore in the final chapter, "Last of the Mohicans": Peter Lim, Cheong Yip Seng and Leslie Fong. Watching how they operated was like sitting through tutorials on a running story on Singapore journalism. I pay my deep respect to them. To Peter, I say "thank you" for showing me how to be a good human being and how to withstand the pressures of government; to Cheong, for displaying how a story can be acutely angled; and to Leslie, for displaying a grit to stay the course in the fight to achieve meaningful journalism despite the great obstacles.

The three women in my life, one wife and two daughters, were very patient as I went silent and grumpy while writing the book. They tolerated a lot of my nonsense and their patience and understanding helped me to complete the book.

One of the first pieces of advice came from a former CNN journalist, Marc Lourdes, who said, after reading my draft of the first chapter: "This is not a journalism article; it is a book, it needs bells and whistles." I never looked back after that.

Ken Jalleh Jr pushed me all the way to rethink some of the chapters. In one case, he was so angry after reading a chapter that he let fly: "Why do you need to bring this incident up after so many years?" I rewrote that chapter substantially and, I must admit, it turned out to be a much better and purposeful chapter. Ken will notice the difference in the "Toh Chin Chye Affair" chapter.

Irene Hoe, my editor, made me rethink words and phrases, pressed me to get my dates and events right and, most importantly, did not flinch to tell me to my face if she did not like what she read. Such editors are rare; we must celebrate them.

And, of course, a "thank you" to Professor Tommy Koh for agreeing to write in his simple, yet inimitable, prose the Foreword on what he felt about the book and the profession called journalism.

Finally, my gratitude to a good friend who went out of his way to help in the research, sometimes at very short notice. There are many more to thank. I appreciate all the words of encouragement, advice and criticisms of the draft chapters. *Reluctant Editor* is richer because of you.

RELUCTANT

EDITOR

CHAPTER 1

My Father's Son
The chapter I didn't want to write

My father, Poravankara Narayanan Nair, was a poet, actor and trade unionist all in one. Our home at Block 9 Room 8, Delhi Road, in the former British Naval Base, doubled as a meeting place and watering hole for my father and his friends to get together to read poetry, discuss the next play to be staged and talk about workers' rights. The discussions were robust, with points and counter-points being argued but seldom reaching a consensus. Still, there was hardly any rancour or bitterness as my father's friends stumbled home. I was a teenager then, barely able to make sense of what prompted these men to debate so animatedly and sometimes wondering if they were just men who were wasting their time drinking and talking about inconsequential things.

Some 60 years later, as I reflect on those days, reality strikes: oh my goodness, how could I have failed to realise that my father's passion for writing, socialism, drama, righteousness, rights of the underdog and his ability to keep going day in day out had rubbed off on me? How I wish that he were alive today! I would have a whisky with him and tell him: "Acha, you made me the man I am today. Thank you very much."

As I was planning the contents of this book, I was adamant that I would not write about my childhood days. Who would care about my growing-up days in the former British Naval Base in Sembawang? Where would people have the time to read about my poverty-stricken early life as my mother struggled daily to put food on the table? In a world where the reader's attention span is shrinking by the day, such chapters are normally given a miss. I have done that many times. My thinking changed as I began working on this book and asked myself: how did I get into journalism? How did I develop a deep interest in Malayalam movies? Where did I get my values from? How did I develop an interest in people from all walks of life? How did I get to writing commentaries that a former Cabinet minister labelled anti-government? How did the hidden empathy for the underdog come out into the open and consume me? I now have the answer: my father's latent influence has played a major part in all of this even without my realisation.

His convictions were powerful and he did not hesitate to express them. Once, my primary school form teacher, Haridass, added the word Nair to my name in my report card. I was registered in school as PN Balji, without the Nair tag. Being a staunch socialist, my father was dead against descriptions like Nair and Menon, which many Malayalees used to show off their class and creed. My father was so pissed off that he stormed into the teachers' room and told Haridass: "Let this caste system end with me. I don't want my children to carry the Nair tag to show that they are from the upper crust of society." Much later, at my engagement ceremony in Singapore in 1974, my father put his foot down with a classy response when asked what kind of dowry he was expecting from the family of my wife to-be, Uma. "Is this a fish market?" he asked, mocking the practice that was prevalent in Indian society. My father-in-law was speechless and no dowry was paid. Struggling to make ends meet, I was upset that my father did not accept the dowry offer. Years later, I was very proud that he did what he did. Now I can say proudly that every dollar and cent that I have has come from my own hard work and from my wife's genius for making good investments.

Somehow, in some way, my father's imprint can be found on many of the decisions I made as editor of *The New Paper*, and then as editor-in-chief of *TODAY* and CEO of Mediacorp Press, which publishes *TODAY*. I didn't realise it at that time; his hidden influence played a part in a high-wire moment when I was the acting editor of the *New Nation* and crossed swords with Lee Kuan Yew over the publication of an article in the paper. Lee Kuan Yew was furious. James Fu, Lee's press secretary, relayed the prime minister's anger to Peter Lim, *The Straits Times* chief editor, in this way: Who is that practising western-style journalism? I was worried that, at best, my progress in the newspaper would be stymied or, at worse, I would lose my job. Nothing happened as Peter managed to pacify Lee. More importantly, I went on to edit *The New Paper* for ten years, and later *TODAY*, for an initial three years and, later on, for another two years. There were many other attempts to walk that tightrope of Singapore journalism, which you can read about in the following pages.

My father's biggest personal disappointment was a month-long strike that he had organised as president of the Naval Base Labour Union. It failed miserably. Years later, when I got my job in the *Malay Mail*, he told me: "Don't ever become a union official." It was advice I have followed religiously. Just as indelible as those words is an image of him that I have carried with me from the early 1980s, when I was about to leave for the US to have an angioplasty done. As I was leaving his home, he pointed a finger at me and said: "Don't forget you have two young girls and a wife to take care of."

My journalism journey also began with my father, long before I became a reporter at the *Malay Mail* on 1 April 1970. He was an avid reader of *The Straits Times*. My brother and I were also hooked on it and so, first thing every morning, there was a race to get to the paper. My father had to step in to restore the peace – the first to rise will get to read the paper first. As always, he would be the first to get up.

We didn't speak much. He was busy with his work and extra-curricular activities. I was busy studying or poaching fruit from the rambutan trees in the backyard of the black and white houses of the British Navy expats.

One day in 1970, he broke the bad news: he was retiring from his job as a storehouse man. My three sisters were married. I had just finished my Higher School Certificate (today's "A" Levels) and my brother was still in secondary school. I had to go out and work to feed the family. I applied for two jobs advertised in *The Straits Times*, one for a reporter in the *Malay Mail*, the other for a special investigator in the Criminal Practices Investigation Bureau (CPIB). Both the *Malay Mail* and the CPIB asked me to attend interviews. Wee Kim Wee, then managing editor of The Straits Times Press, in whose stable the *Malay Mail* was parked, headed the interview panel, and the human resource person made me an offer almost immediately. The salary was S$250 with a transport allowance of S$50. The CPIB called me a few days later asking me to join them, but with my dream job in hand, the CPIB was the last thing on my mind. I walked into Times House in Kim Seng Road (where a condominium now stands in place of Times House) with a swagger in my gait and confidence in my head – only for both the swagger and confidence to be punctured a few days later.

The cause was my news editor, Jackie Sam, who revelled in being a tyrant. He made life hell for me and many others. Jackie brought to life the caricatures of editors made famous by Hollywood: smoking endlessly, trying to look for something on his table hidden by piles of files with paper chucked all over, barking orders to journalists ... Jackie epitomised this kind of behaviour. Once, he sent me to interview a Big Walk participant in a kampong in Bukit Timah. I wrote up the interview, he had a quick look at my report and asked me to go back and talk to the subject again. Nothing was said about what was missing in the story or the extra questions I needed to ask. I went back and back and back ... 12 times. He must have decided then that the punishment was enough and he finally rewrote the story for publication. No explanations, no suggestions, no empathy. It was a far better story than what I had written. It was crisp, short and flowed smoothly. That whole episode was intended as an exercise in humiliation and it worked. Enough was enough. I threw in my letter of resignation. It landed on the chief reporter's desk because Jackie happened to be off that day and a veteran newsman, PM Raman, was in charge. He called me at home and said: "I am chucking your letter into the bin. Come back to work." Raman was like a father figure in the *Malay Mail* newsroom, offering a shoulder to cry on for those who got a verbal lashing from Jackie or one of his cold, piercing trademark stares. I couldn't go against the advice of the avuncular Raman.

Together with police inspector-turned-reporter Wee Beng Huat, I was made to do a punishing shift from 11pm to 8am, followed by a week on the 3am to 11am shift. Beng Huat and I would make regular visits to the Singapore General Hospital mortuary, meet officers of the Fire Brigade and talk to his police contacts. It was at around this time that the *Singapore Herald*, anchored by media stalwarts such as Francis Wong and Ambrose Khaw, came on the scene. The *Herald* began putting pressure on *The Straits Times* from the word go. *Herald* exclusives and stories that angered the government made many sit up. I remember a picture that was used across a full page inside the paper with this cheeky headline: "The picture the government doesn't want you to see." Below it was a picture of a military contingent practising its National Day marchpast on a public road. The government had ordered the media not to use the picture as they felt that it would dilute the people's enjoyment of the actual parade.

The *Herald*'s Harold Soh, another police officer turned crime reporter, was getting stories which we could not even smell. Then we found out he was rewarding those who manned the telephone lines of the Fire Brigade, the first people to receive 999 calls. Our relationship with the telephone operators had cooled and the tip-offs dried up. Not wanting the *Herald* team to beat us to the crime stories, we also started rewarding the 999 operators and our relationship returned to "normal", until one day when we were meeting them in a coffee shop in Chinatown, CPIB officers barged in and arrested all of us. We were packed off to the CPIB office in Stamford Road, isolated in separate cold rooms and interrogated for nearly 20 hours. It was a totally numbing experience. On one level, I was thinking of my job, whether I would still be able to continue in journalism. On another level, I was thinking of how I was going to face my parents and society. Beng Huat and I spent a lot of time at MacRitchie Reservoir, crying on each other's shoulders. A few months later, we both pleaded guilty to corruption and were fined $1,000 each. The telephone operators were all sacked. That incident never left me, piercing at my conscience every time I think about it. We didn't lose our jobs, but the telephone operators did.

This is it, I told myself. I didn't want to do reporting any more. Fortunately, I got moved to the sub-editor's desk. That was where I found my true calling.

CHAPTER 2

Accidental Sub-editor, Reluctant Editor
In a world of tabloids

Most of my 35 years in mainstream journalism was lived in the world of the media underdog. Except for a five-year spell (1982–1988) in *The Straits Times* (ST), I worked for tabloids that had to kick and punch to stay above water. Success was never a sure thing. Every day was a battle of wits, reporting and shaping news stories, knowing full well that the mighty ST almost always commanded first bite, leaving the minnows like us to fight over the crumbs. ST was like a towering banyan tree in whose suffocating shade lesser plants might sometimes steal enough sunlight to survive, but never enough to overshadow the big banyan. The four tabloids I worked for – *Malay Mail*, *New Nation*, *The New Paper* and *TODAY* – had to rely on their reporters' intuitive ability and agility to deliver exclusives, and on their editors' creative presentation of stories to whet readers' appetites to buy the newspapers day after day. The journalists' survival instincts were tested every publishing day.

At *The New Paper*, one of the several consultants who had come from US News & World Report was the avuncular Don Reeder, who worked with reporters to make their stories meaningful and reader friendly. One day, I asked Don what he made of the paper. He said:

> I go back home every evening not knowing what the paper is going to look like. The next morning, I am surprised to see a well-edited, well-designed and lively paper. I don't know how you all pull it off. Obviously, there is a central intelligence running through the newsroom and the paper. Keep doing whatever you are doing.

My turning point in tabloid journalism came in the 1970s, when I was a crime reporter with the *New Nation*. Colleague Wee Beng Huat and I were caught and fined for bribing the Fire Brigade's telephone operators to get tip-offs on crime stories. I have wondered many times how my career would have turned out if not for that episode. The conviction in a court of law was so traumatic that I wanted to quit reporting immediately. When the management agreed to move me to sub-editing, I took to the new role with great enthusiasm and relish. The desk-bound job of sub-editing and laying out pages for the newspaper suited my introverted nature. No longer did I have to station myself at the Singapore General Hospital mortuary every working night to interview grieving relatives and hang around hospitals to see ambulances bringing in blood-stained victims of accidents and murders.

My move to the sub-editor's desk at the *New Nation* coincided with the arrival of a Sri Lankan, Maurice Perera. His professionalism, meticulousness, commitment, perseverance and sheer appetite for hard work struck me immediately. Watching him in action was like looking at an artist adding a stroke here and a shade there. He worked with hardly a complaint. I decided that he was the journalist I wanted to emulate. At our paper, which was targeted to reach the streets by noon, sub-editors generally arrived by 5am and would leave by lunch time. Maurice would go home only when he was satisfied with the final version of the pages he had laid out. Most days, that meant he would be in the office until 6pm. I was fortunate that he took a liking to me. As my unofficial mentor, he taught me the finer points of sub-editing and page layout. It was his habit to collect some of the most effective layouts he came across in British newspapers. He would meticulously file them under such headings as murder, politics and personality interviews, and refer to them regularly, adapting the ideas in those tear sheets to his own layouts. I followed his lead and kept my own collection on topics of interest for many years.

Khoo Teng Soon was at one time Singapore's best page designer. In the industry, he was better known as TS Khoo, and "The Fastest Pen In The East" for the pace at which he could turn out great pages. He was group editor of The Straits Times Press (1975) Ltd throughout most of the 1970s. One day, I fished out of the newsroom bin his working layouts for the next day's front page of ST. I put them side by side on a table to see how that final Page One had evolved. Like an instruction manual, they provided useful insights into his thinking and the principles he applied. It was like learning at the feet of a silent sage, trying to make sense of the transformation of the front page from its inception, through the preliminary layouts and into the masterful final.

It would be impossible not to mention David Kraal, the editor of *New Nation*. He was the very antithesis of the Brahmin editors of that era, the high priests of the printed page, who lorded it over the newsrooms as if they were God's gift to journalism. That aside, they were true professionals, masters of their trade. Whether laying out pages, writing headlines or turning around complex stories on difficult issues to make them digestible, they were a joy to observe, study and emulate. David had all those skills. Unlike them, though, he was approachable, always there, constantly listening to his staff and trying to help them professionally and personally. He threw some difficult and exciting pages at me, this accidental sub-editor. I discussed them with Maurice and began to realise that this was what I wanted to do in journalism. Sitting quietly in one corner of the newsroom, stroking my beard, going out for a walk when I needed to clear my mind ... this job suited me to a T.

I rose up the editorial ladder and became acting editor in 1981, a year before we had to give up the *New Nation* title and break up our newsroom. The layoffs that followed were especially difficult and bitter because it was not only the group and ST that were very profitable at the time, but even our *New Nation* was just beginning to turn in a small profit.

Fate, this time by the name of Lee Kuan Yew (LKY), intervened in an unthinkable way to turn my life, and those of many, upside down. LKY had initiated the creation of a rival to ST, so as to challenge the paper to up its game and to provide what he saw as the waning Chinese-language newspaper industry with an English-language lifeline to the future. However, the newbie, the *Singapore Monitor*, was taking way too long to get off the starting blocks because of disagreements between its editorial and corporate bosses. LKY stepped in to broker a corporate deal, by getting the *New Nation* to hand over its masthead to the *Monitor* in 1982. All the advertising contracts that the *New Nation* had secured were passed over to the *Monitor*. LKY sweetened the deal by letting *New Nation*'s owner, The Straits Times Press, take a stake in the Chinese-language *Shin Min Daily News*. With that behind-the-scenes manoeuvre, a new paper to rival ST was born and a sacrificial lamb dispatched. This move by LKY would have been unthinkable anywhere else in the industry but it fitted into his grand scheme to make sure that ST remained relevant and the dominant player in Singapore's media scene. That move became a prelude to the merger of the country's newspapers into Singapore Press Holdings (SPH) in 1984.

To LKY, ST was like a porcelain vase that had to be protected and nurtured at all costs. That was what he famously told SR Nathan, when he asked Nathan, the career public servant, to become executive chairman of SPH. LKY knew the value of ST as his propaganda machine, but he was also sensitive to the paper's need to get Singaporeans to read and support it. He made sure it had no competition, allowing the paper to make lots of money, but he realised that the downside of a lack of competition was a possible slide in standards and a loss of readership, and so the *Monitor* was finally born.

In anticipation of what was to come, ST went into a take-no-prisoners battle mode, signing exclusive arrangements with international media organisations to use their materials, even their comics. The publishing giant's circulation and advertising departments made sure that the *Monitor* would run up against huge and never-ending hurdles. One ST tactic was to send its circulation staff to newsagents and pile copies of ST on top of those of the *Monitor*, tricking would-be buyers into thinking that the tabloid was not available.

The newbie struggled. It lacked an experienced and crafty CEO who understood how the Singapore market worked. It was not long before the red ink began to colour the balance sheets and the new venture began staring into an abyss of deepening losses and feeble circulation gains. Its financial backer, United Overseas Bank, realising that there was no prospect of a quick turnaround, pulled the plug in 1985, a scant three years after its birth.

Editorially, the *Monitor* had been a breath of fresh air in what some may have considered a staid, even stale, media scene in Singapore. When the *Monitor*'s death was announced, a group of students from the National University of Singapore wanted to gather support for a new newspaper to rival ST. The president of the Students' Political Association, Tan Tnng Nuan, said at that time: "We are concerned about the closure of the *Monitor*. The closure has led to a vacuum, with one newspaper and one opinion."

The demise of the original *New Nation* on 30 June 1982, one year after I became acting editor, was a sad day for the staff. The paper was respected for its reports, analyses and commentaries as they were well received by many readers. Some of its writers became talking points in a Singapore where journalists were unlikely candidates for celebrity status. Ismail Kassim's reports and analyses from Malaysia were closely followed on both sides of the Causeway, with his keen observations of Dr Mahathir Mohamad's controversial decisions communicated by fax machine to readers up north. Education correspondent Teresa Ooi's commentaries and exclusives always got the attention of teachers – and almost as often got on the nerves of the Education Ministry. Never far from controversy, sports writer Jeffrey Low's Malaysia Cup analyses often became the subject of intense lunch-time debate and Tan Bah Bah's editorials were scrutinised by the government with a fine toothcomb. Said Bah Bah:

> Despite the presence of Big Brother, we at *New Nation* pounded away producing stories that many government agencies didn't like. Press freedom was practised except that none of us was carrying placards.

Working behind the scenes in planning and shaping the reports were stalwarts like Sonny Yap, who went about his work as features editor calmly and methodically, without any high jinks. He spoke of what he got from working in *New Nation*:

> Immeasurable. A grounding in journalism which is unreplicable in today's newsrooms; exposure to the gritty Singapore of the 1970s; lessons from editors and seniors which stay with me to this day. Then there were the myriad training programmes and overseas sabbaticals which made up for my lack of higher education. Not to mention the career breaks and opportunities which enabled me to grow in my job.

A gritty Singapore indeed. Still reeling from a shock exit in 1965 from Malaysia, just two years after a ground-breaking merger, Singapore was struck by a second thunderbolt – the withdrawal of British troops east of Suez in 1971. The economic and political fallout of these events was huge, especially for a newly-independent Singapore. The troops were a £70-million annual burden on the British economy which the then Labour government decided it could no longer bear. To Singapore, the British bases were a boon, contributing 20 per cent to the GDP. The quickie divorce from Malay-dominated Malaysia was the result of an intractable divide over race, and came in the wake of public sparring between leaders north and south of the Causeway. It sparked fears of a revival of the 1964 racial riots. Those events gave LKY the perfect opportunity to use the

Internal Security Act to arrest certain opposition politicians, including union leaders, without trial. With the opposition neutralised, the country embarked on rapid industrialisation, changed labour laws to attract foreign investments and tripled military spending. Nearly everything we see in today's Singapore – whether it is the glittering prosperity of the city state or the paucity of political space – has its roots in how LKY and his lieutenants dealt with that double whammy.

ST was a huge beneficiary of the dazzling economic growth. As the country prospered, so did ST. Strict media licensing laws and the government-enforced closure of its rivals, *Eastern Sun* and the *Singapore Herald*, also helped ST and its parent company to become runaway economic successes. They paid back the favour by supporting the government unabashedly, sometimes even if it meant disregarding the most important stakeholder – the reader. LKY's strategy for ensuring ST's loyalty worked well for both parties from the late 1970s.

Lyn Holloway and Peter Lim used the opportunity to launch the golden era for Singapore journalists. Both the CEO and editor-in-chief came up with plans to upgrade journalists' professional, leadership and intellectual skills. The icing on the cake was the initiative to give senior editors a two-week sabbatical of their choice to anywhere every year. Even their wives' flight tickets were paid for. I asked Peter why the company was so generous. He reasoned: our senior editors work long hours, this was our small way of saying "thank you" to the wives. He was disappointed that he couldn't convince the board to extend it to the husbands of female editors. Peter and Lyn also made it a point to send flowers on the wedding anniversaries of the senior editors and their spouses. Peter intervened personally to get the company to grant me a housing loan (the company had no such loan scheme). He also got the company to underwrite my travel expenses and medical bills when I had an angioplasty done in San Francisco in 1986, although SPH's executive chairman at the time, SR Nathan, had not been in favour of it since the procedure was already available in Singapore.

The Lyn Holloway-Peter Lim tango effectively skirted the barrier between the corporate and editorial departments and I have not seen that partnership repeated since. Peter knew he had to get the buy-in of the CEO to retain and attract talent, and Lyn had the foresight to realise that editorial excellence would boost readership and advertising revenue. Like all good things, this arrangement didn't last. Soon after, ex-Cabinet minister Lim Kim San replaced SR Nathan as SPH's executive chairman in 1988; he slashed executives' perks, unceremoniously ending the golden era.

Most of the *New Nation*'s staff moved to ST after our newspaper was gifted to the *Singapore Monitor* in 1982. My five years in ST, beginning in 1982, were difficult. I held important roles, including those of night editor and news editor, but found it hard to adjust to a newsroom so radically different from the ones I had known. ST was much more hierarchical and disciplined. I was a fish out of water trying to swim through a labyrinth of rules. ST had little choice but to keep a tight rein on the newsroom, with an ever-watchful and ever-suspicious officialdom scrutinising its reports; one misjudgement might lead to an internal inquiry, a rap on the knuckles and perhaps force the company to move certain journalists to other departments. So when SPH management announced that a new paper would be launched in 1988, I jumped at the chance of a transfer. Editor-in-chief Cheong Yip Seng agreed and I was made deputy to the chief editor, Peter

Lim, who had to resign as editor-in-chief in charge of the English and Malay newspapers under SPH.

The working title was Project 459, supposedly representing the first three digits of telephone numbers in Toa Payoh, a neighbourhood whose metrics matched those of our target audience. To reach these readers, our stories would be short and snappy, and its photographs and illustrations would be in colour – a big deal then as colour tended to be reserved for National Day and other special occasions. Each edition would feature a glossary, giving the meanings of certain words that appeared in the stories. Mock-ups were shown to potential advertisers and readers.

The marketplace buzz and much of the feedback were supportive, but when the first copies of *The New Paper* (TNP) rolled off the presses on 26 July 1988, the reaction was just the opposite. Clearly, Singapore was not ready for a paper that treated news in a catchy and fun way. Giordano showed its displeasure by cancelling its advertising contract and the paper's sales sank below 50,000 copies a day, much below expectations. Peter acted quickly. The paper went downmarket, with sensational Page One headlines. One year after the launch, TNP ran a series of stories on a prostitute in the UK who counted among her clients famous newspaper editors and British MPs. The series became an instant hit and Pamella Bordes – nicknamed Papadum Pam because of her Indian origins – became a talking point because of the treatment of the story, revealing salacious details of her life story. Other stories followed in a similar vein and the paper's circulation began to breach the 50,000 figure. Like an experienced pilot, Peter was readying the paper for take-off after a false start.

However, SPH executive chairman Lim Kim San was not happy. He reckoned that our staff costs were too high because of the highly-paid western journalists in the TNP newsroom. Peter's own pay and perks were a constant source of irritation for the chairman. He hounded Peter often. In 1990, two years after the launch, Peter decided to leave. He asked me if I would take over as editor, but I was reluctant as I was worried about my health. I had only recently returned to work after an angioplasty procedure in the US and believed that taking on the top job would be too much for my heart. Peter took me to lunch in a small and charming restaurant called Checkers in Orchard Road to persuade me. I left the decision to my wife, Uma, as it would mean I would have even less time to spend at home. She took three days to make up her mind and told me to go ahead and accept the job.

I did, and my ten years as editor of TNP turned out to be the best experience that I had in my career. The paper hit new highs in circulation, helped mainly by breaking news from Operation Desert Shield, the build-up to the first Gulf War which was launched in August 1990, and the outbreak of the war itself in January 1991. The 1990 World Cup in Italy was another rocket booster as most of the football matches during that miracle month in June and July were played early in the morning, Singapore time. TNP became the Singapore newspaper to get the first bite of the news from Italia 90. Readers began to lap up the breaking news, analyses and action graphics, and the paper's sales began to soar, hitting a daily peak of 150,000.

TNP became my university of life, with my personality seeing a transformation. I had always been an impossible introvert, speaking very little and seldom socialising with colleagues. During meetings, I was mostly silent, speaking only when spoken to. My ten-year editorship of TNP changed all that. I forced myself to go out and mingle with people. I accepted invitations to speak at public functions, and I regularly convened newsroom-wide meetings. Bit by bit, I began to break out of my cocoon. TNP's success made the transformation easier. Editor-in-chief, Cheong Yip Seng, became a catalyst. He believed in TNP, attended nearly every Tuesday meeting with the editors, praised the paper publicly and endorsed it many times. All this gave me the much-needed confidence to break out of my introverted, shy and even reticent personality. Many times, I swung to the other extreme, becoming very talkative (too talkative, says my wife, Uma).

TNP gave me a rich understanding of various aspects of publishing. SPH's chief operating officer, Denis Tay, took a special interest in the paper, chairing a weekly meeting of the heads of the editorial, marketing and circulation departments. Those meetings, where all the departments had to present reports on TNP's progress and follow-up plans, were instructive as they plucked me out of my narrow editorial concerns and made me acknowledge and understand that the success of a newspaper depended on all three departments coming together regularly to share information on what the market wanted. It was from the circulation briefings that I learnt the most. Its staff was out there on the streets, mingling with readers and newspaper vendors informally. They had the pulse of the reader; they knew what readers looked for in an afternoon newspaper, why some editions sold well, why others didn't. Their briefings were more art than science; I learnt not to ask them questions because they saw that as editorial arrogance and shied away from being open and candid. Our relationship grew; they had no inhibitions about telling me whether an edition would sell well just by looking at the headlines and pictures on Page One. They never sugar-coated their judgements, and most times, they were spot on. The newsroom would fax the Page One layouts to them daily.

Meanwhile, I had to deal with a strongman executive chairman who repeatedly threatened to shut us down if we didn't show him we were committed to reducing the red ink on our balance sheet. To show him that we were on the right track, when journalists resigned, we simply reallocated the work and did not replace them. Soon, Lim Kim San got off our backs and that removed a big obstacle to our take-off.

My TNP life was my most rewarding newspaper experience, not just because it became the only afternoon daily to hit a daily sales figure of more than 100,000 copies a day, but also because of the talented team of editors, sub-editors, reporters, artists and administrative staff I worked with. They thrived in an open newsroom environment that was not straight-jacketed. It spawned a crazy and wild bunch who played and worked hard and helped make TNP a talking point. I must make a special mention of editorial artists such as Cel Gulapa, Lee Hup Kheng and Simon Ang; writers and editors, including T Ramakrishan, R Jegathesan, Ken Jalleh Jr, Ng Whay Hock, Joe Nathan Lourdes, Pradeep Paul, Suresh Nair, Yaw Yan Chong, Pauline Loh, Irene Ng and Rosnah Ahmad; photographers like Philip Lim, Simon Ker and Jonathan Choo, and admin staff, including Zainah Omar and R Nirmala. It was a dream team of world-class professionals – some of them are still making waves in their new roles both inside and outside the newsroom.

CHAPTER 3

Living Dangerously

Who is that practising western-style journalism?

Nearly every editor in Singapore has a Lee Kuan Yew story to tell. Former editor-in-chief, Cheong Yip Seng, has written in his book, OB Markers: My Straits Times Story,[1] of being warned as a rookie reporter that if he broke an embargo, he would have his neck broken. That was in the 1960s. Peter Lim, his immediate predecessor at Singapore Press Holdings, has told us about how he was made to hand over the New Nation title to a rival newspaper company; and former Straits Times editor, Leslie Fong, of how he nearly lost his job over his "Thinking Aloud" column.

My own Lee Kuan Yew story began on 3 February 1981, 11 years after I first entered the newsroom in Times House. It was the eve of Chinese New Year and I was then acting editor of the afternoon daily, the New Nation. That day, the Chinese-language papers had a report on Prime Minister Lee Kuan Yew's Chinese New Year message, which had been released for publication exclusively to the local Chinese-language media. Other media had to wait until the next day to receive the message

---

[1] Cheong Yip Seng, OB Markers: My Straits Times Story (Straits Times Press, 2012).

for publication the day after. The first day of this public holiday was one of two days in the whole year when the *New Nation* was the only English-language newspaper to be published, the other being Boxing Day. *New Nation* journalists made sure that those special editions were memorable, with stories that would encourage readers to buy the paper regularly.

The message from the Prime Minister did not just contain festive wishes for the new year, it carried a compelling news point of national significance. The Housing and Development Board (HDB), the national housing authority, was looking at ways to get public housing residents to live near their parents in the same estate. The political and social impact of his message was impossible to ignore. The natural expansion of HDB housing was splintering Singapore families. With ageing citizens preferring to stay put as their adult children married and moved into homes in newer estates, it seemed inevitable that over time, such separation on a national scale would weaken family ties. Unintended though it was, it would inevitably result in seniors leading lonely lives and, eventually, the state would be required to look after them.

A *New Nation* editor called the Prime Minister's press secretary, James Fu, and was told about the embargo, which reserved publication for the Chinese-language newspapers as they did not publish on the first and second days of the Chinese New Year. Fu said they would release it to the rest of the media one day later, on the first day of the Chinese New Year, for publication the next day. Such a rule seemed strange to me, especially when news of the HDB's plan was already in the public domain, albeit only in Chinese. Fu was adamant that the *New Nation* respect this two-stage embargo. I appealed, but he refused to budge. Finally, I heeded my journalistic instincts and went ahead with publishing the story on the first day of the Chinese New Year.

The *New Nation*'s report, "Bringing Families Together", said:[2]

> Mr Lee discussed the problem of parents who are unwilling to move to a new housing estate and who would rather their children apply for a flat in their estate. Unfortunately, he said, this cannot be easily done because the old estates have been fully developed and those blocks that are being rebuilt will not be enough to accommodate such applicants. He suggested that the HDB make it more attractive, in terms of price, for the exchange and resale of old flats. Mr Lee said he was shocked to discover during a tour of Ang Mo Kio on Jan 25 that there are two old folks' homes in the estate. He said this is something we should not encourage.

Within minutes of the paper hitting the streets, the Prime Minister's Office called. Peter Lim, who had editorial oversight of the *New Nation*, got the brunt of the scolding. Fu relayed the Prime Minister's angry message: "Who is that journalist practising western-style journalism?" Through the press secretary, Peter tried to pacify the Prime Minister by explaining that I was new to the role of editor and did not know it was accepted practice for the government to grant the first bite of the Chinese New Year message to the Chinese-language press. Although I was acting on the journalistic principle that it was acceptable to publish information that was already in the public domain, I came to realise that I ought to have checked with the editor-in-chief

---

[2] "Bringing Families Together", *New Nation*, 4 February 1981, page 1.

before deciding to go ahead. This episode, however, had a happy ending: the CEO of the newspaper company, Lyn Holloway, later walked into my room, put his arm around my shoulders and said: "Don't worry, Balji. We have taken care of it." That act of warmth and support has stayed with me ever since. I had expected the worst. Lee Kuan Yew was known to be intolerant of dissent, especially from those working in media. His record with journalists who veered off the straight and narrow path was legendary. Some have been detained without trial, some blackballed, and others forced to leave journalism and even the country. My worst fear about getting into his bad books was that I might be forced to quit journalism altogether. None of this materialised. Not only did I continue to run the *New Nation* until 1982 when we had to gift it to our competitor, Singapore News and Publications Ltd, but I also edited *The New Paper* for ten years from 1990 to 2000 and launched *TODAY* as the founding editor-in-chief and CEO of Mediacorp Press, its publisher. That stint lasted three years until 2003.

My colleague of many years, Mary Lee, was not so fortunate. She had been a writer for *The Singapore Herald* newspaper, which was forced to close in 1971. Accused of being part of a "black ops" plot mounted by foreigners, the newspaper had its publishing licence suspended. Lee Kuan Yew had accused the *Herald* of "taking the government on" since it began publication in 1970. Weeks before its closure, another English-language daily, *Eastern Sun*, had also been forced to close. Government action against the media was not confined to English-language publications. The Chinese-language *Nanyang Siang Pau* was accused of glamourising communism and encouraging Chinese chauvinism. Publication of the paper was suspended briefly and four of its editorial executives were detained for up to two years.

After the *Herald* episode, Mary went to the US on a journalism fellowship, then joined the *Sunday Nation* team upon her return. She got on the Prime Minister's nerves from the very first day in November 1974. She became the target of his fury because of her "provocative" columns; that was how the paper's editor, Cheong Yip Seng, described them publicly. One commentary that infuriated Lee Kuan Yew was headlined "The Great Paper Chase". He wanted Mary sacked for saying that the pursuit of certificates and degrees was a total waste of time. He felt that she was undermining the education system. Peter Lim, who was the *New Nation*'s chief editor at that time, and Cheong tried to appease the Prime Minister by moving Mary to a back-end job as a sub-editor. "I wasn't happy but neither was I living in fear then," she would recall in a 2013 article, "How LKY Changed My Life", on the Singapore news website, *The Independent*. It was during the difficult period in the 1970s that a former classmate, who had not been in touch for seven years, took her on a car ride so they could talk privately. Be careful, he told her. Throw out all publications you brought back from the US. Don't invite to your home anyone you are not familiar with, and don't hold any parties in your place, he advised.

"It wasn't pleasant. Suddenly, I'm no longer able to trust anyone around me, except my mother. I cried for days. I knew what I had to do: I had to leave Singapore," Mary wrote. At the time, she was a writer at the paper, handpicked by Cheong to work with him on the *Sunday Nation*.

Some felt Cheong should have taken responsibility because he had approved her commentaries and promoted her as a provocative columnist. In a newsroom that felt under siege, journalists turned fearful, figuratively – and sometimes literally – looking behind their backs and self-censoring their own work. Those close to Mary knew that her free-spiritedness and her uncompromising views on current affairs would make her a target in Lee Kuan Yew's Singapore. Leaving her country of birth would be an eventuality.

In 1975, she left for London, with no money and no idea of what she would do there. Mary depended on her friends until she got a job at Harrods as a sales assistant during the Christmas season. Then she went into journalism working as a sub-editor at a weekly newspaper, did some casual work at *The Sunday Times* and was taken on as a sub-editor by *The Guardian*. Two years later, she landed a job in Hong Kong with the *Far Eastern Economic Review* magazine. There, she was in her element ("full of adventure," she wrote) writing commentaries as a correspondent in Beijing and an open letter to Lee Kuan Yew, headlined "Lee To Lee", which was a sharp criticism of Lee Kuan Yew's stranglehold on Singapore society. "Ease your hold on Singapore and in 25 years' time, the island will have grown into a real garden city where a hundred more flowers – some wild, but all beautiful – will bloom naturally," she wrote. That was in 1985. As expected, the advice was not followed and today's leadership is struggling to find ways to allow the wild flowers to bloom.

Mary returned to Singapore in 1995 for "medical and personal reasons". The *Far Eastern Economic Review* kept her on salary for a couple of years as an "observer". She earned a Master's degree in English, then applied to Singapore Press Holdings for a job. The interview panel was divided. Mano Sabnani, then managing editor of the English and Malay newspapers division, was in favour of hiring her, saying that people, especially experienced journalists, should be given a second chance. The HR people were not, citing her commentaries and her controversial run-ins with the government. The ball was kicked into my court for a decision and I took Mano's side. Cheong, who was now editor-in-chief, concurred, and Mary returned to her old Times House haunt, this time as a sub-editor with *The New Paper*, after an absence of 20 years.

Initially, it was smooth going in a newsroom that embraced Mary's seniority, knowledge of Asia and ability to cut through the clutter in reports written by young reporters. She played the role of mother hen perfectly, feeding staff with her homemade *kueh pie tee* and providing a listening ear. Her rebellious instincts, however, did show up occasionally and finally caught fire when the BBC sought her views on Singapore's ministerial salaries, which made its politicians the world's highest paid. She could hardly have chosen a more controversial topic. Mary told the BBC interviewer: "It was OK to pay basketball star Michael Jordan millions because his skills were self-evident. But ministers? Their skills, if they had any, can't be seen." Ouch!

Lee Kuan Yew was not going to keep quiet about that. The salaries idea was his brainchild and he was hell-bent on paying ministers top dollar because he said he was having problems getting good people into politics. He demolished all criticism and the very subject became an OB (out-of-bounds) marker, an issue that was not for discussion. Even a quarter of a century later, ministerial pay remains an issue that polarises Singapore society. It was on 21 October 1994 that the White Paper on Competitive Salaries for Competent and Honest Government was presented to Parliament. The central argument that high salaries were needed to recruit talent was not generally disputed, but it was the amount of money being proposed, making Singapore politicians the world's highest paid, that many could not accept. The media was given specific instructions not to report the increments that were given every year to the ministers for fear that putting that kind of information in the public domain would reignite acrimonious debate and stoke public anger.

Mary's BBC interview ran smack into the government's take-no-prisoners stance on the issue. Lee Kuan Yew's reaction came fast and furious and, once again, he wanted action taken against her. An internal inquiry panel recommended that she be told to go. That decision rested on a company rule that she had broken: she had failed to seek the editor's permission to give that interview. *The New Paper* appealed to Cheong Yip Seng, who agreed on a compromise: Mary would be demoted and her salary cut.

Back in 1981, *The Straits Times* (ST) had done something uncharacteristic and unthinkable. It had responded publicly to Communications and Labour Minister Ong Teng Cheong, who criticised ST and the *New Nation* for publishing what he called "irresponsible, misleading and rumour-mongering" reports on impending bus fare increases. The reports said the bus company was mulling over two proposals: the price of bus concession passes to go up between $1 and $10, and a general fare increase of 5 cents.

The reporters attributed the information to unnamed sources. The group editor, Peter Lim, went public with a spirited defence of the newspapers and their reporters, something I have not witnessed since. Such debates had taken place privately between Cabinet ministers and editors occasionally, but never in public.

As acting editor of the *New Nation*, I was required to attend an unusual press conference that Ong Teng Cheong had called to deny the reports, in the presence of key ministry officials and Singapore Bus Service (SBS) bosses. Visibly upset, the minister looked directly at the editors assembled on the opposite side of the table and said in a dramatic tone of voice: "All the reliable sources you can lay your hands on are here. Name them." The line-up included Permanent Secretary (Communications) Sim Kee Boon, and from SBS managing director Tan Kong Eng, executive director Lim Leong Geok and general manager Mah Bow Tan.[3]

At that tense confrontation over the bus fare hike reports, one of the unnamed sources cited by the newspapers was seated there right in front of us, his expression impassive. Peter Lim declined to expose him, saying that professional ethics prevented him from naming our sources. Peter went further when he said the sources who provided the information were authoritative but conceded they had now proven unreliable.

One heart-stopping moment came as the press conference was winding up. Peter noticed that Sim Kee Boon, the Permanent Secretary, appeared lost in thought. Peter asked him: "You have something else on your mind, Mr Sim?" Sim Kee Boon said he wondered if *The Straits Times* would give an apology. Peter asked: "Is one called for?" Sim Kee Boon felt that in view of what had been established, an apology might not be out of place. Peter said

---

[3] Mah Bow Tan would later enter politics and join the Cabinet, holding the Communications, Environment and National Development portfolios in the course of a 27-year political career, before quitting Parliament in 2015.

he would give the suggestion his serious consideration. In the end, no apology was given.

This was actually the second confrontation between the minister and Peter Lim; the first had come the day before when Ong Teng Cheong slammed the English-language press over their reports on this issue, at an event attended by Chinese-language newspaper reporters. In the ST report the next day, headlined "Teng Cheong Raps *Straits Times* And *New Nation*", Peter had already made clear what the group's response would be. He said: "If *New Nation* and *The Straits Times* were to name their sources, no one, not even Mr Ong, we think, would feel that the two newspapers had been irresponsible."

In the course of writing this chapter, I caught up with Rav Dhaliwal, the *New Nation* reporter who had written the story of the bus fare increase, and asked who her sources were. She gave me two names. I then asked her why they had leaked the story to the press. She said: "As the controversy blew up, I realised that the information was leaked to test the ground. They wanted to see how the ground would react. If the reaction was negative, then they would announce a substantially lower increase. Yes, we were used by these two people for their devious means."

That long-ago government face-off with the media was a rare moment when I was proud to be a Singapore journalist. When Peter made the issue public and responded in a firm but gentlemanly way, he showed all of us journalists how the media could respond when it felt it had been unjustifiably reprimanded by the government. I remember him telling senior editors that if we had done something wrong, we should come clean, admit our mistake and apologise. If not, we should forward our case unemotionally and in a balanced manner.

Much later, we would learn that this episode had negative consequences for Ong Teng Cheong's political prospects. A new generation of leaders was being groomed to take over from Lee Kuan Yew and his team. Ong was a key member of that second tier and this perceived setback was seen as one reason he failed to become Singapore's second prime minister. He was also the go-to minister for matters relating to the Chinese community. While he focused his attack on the English-language newspapers, no mention was made of *Nanyang Siang Pau*, which was the first newspaper to report that bus fares would go up. When asked by *The Straits Times* why the English media had been singled out, Ong Teng Cheong said he had spoken to *Nanyang Siang Pau*'s editor-in-chief and registered his unhappiness. Some political observers saw that as a leadership weakness in an aspiring national leader and wondered if he could truly be a leader of all races.

More importantly, there was the question of how Lee Kuan Yew would have regarded the whole episode. Some Singaporeans feel that Lee Kuan Yew, who believed that editors had to be tamed at all cost, would have seen this as a weakness in Ong Teng Cheong. Ultimately, it was Goh Chok Tong who succeeded Lee Kuan Yew as Prime Minister in 1990, and Ong became Deputy Prime Minister (DPM). Ong Teng Cheong's appointment as DPM was referred to in the book, *Tall Order*.[4] When Goh Chok Tong told Lee Kuan Yew of his intention to pick Ong, Lee Kuan Yew asked why his son, Lee Hsien Loong, was not on the list. Goh Chok Tong got around that sticky situation by appointing two DPMs – Ong Teng Cheong and Lee Hsien Loong.

---

[4] Peh Shing Huei, *Tall Order – The Goh Chok Tong Story* (World Scientific, 2018).

In 1991, I was involved in another tangle with the government, again over sources. *The New Paper*'s ace crime reporter, Suresh Nair, had gotten hold of a report that detailed a Super Puma crash at Sembawang Air Base, which took the lives of four crew members. The statement issued by the Ministry of Defence (Mindef) was brief, as usual. It offered scant details, such as the name of the aircraft, where and when the accident happened and how many died. Through his sources, Suresh dug up more information, including the likely cause of the crash (malfunction of the rear rotor blades) and the pilot losing control of the chopper after it suddenly spun mid-flight. The report quoted sources as saying: "The pilot informed the control tower that he was facing some mechanical problems when cruising between 250 and 350 metres."

We did not realise that we were contravening Mindef secrecy laws. Many months later, Suresh learnt that an investigation had been ordered to find out who had leaked the story. "Between six and eight of my sources who offered the technical information were pulled up by military intelligence and interrogated for several days at the Bukit Gombak Base," he said. Permanent Secretary (Defence) Lim Siong Guan demanded that we name the sources. Suresh and I declined because revealing those names was as good as killing our profession. Lim listened, did not say much and we left that meeting thinking the matter was settled. Until we were called in a second time. Again, Lim asked us for the names of the sources, and again, we declined. We were told that we would be charged in court for contravening Mindef regulations. In the end, that never came to pass. Instead, we were fined via private summons. Suresh recalled: "I was told that some officers and non-commissioned officers who were questioned were punished with demotions, salary cuts and a salary freeze. The incident pains me even today, 27 years later, that my buddies who risked their careers to give me such exclusive information were punished severely."

It taught me a meaningful lesson. The details published in our report had been too close for Mindef's comfort and left no doubt that the information had been leaked from the airbase. Not only would an employer find such a leak intolerable, but the law was also clearly against us. If the team had better understood the ramifications of the law, we could have handled the details differently and the chances of Mindef coming down hard on the paper would have been minimised, and the officers involved might not have had to pay such a heavy price.

Suresh belonged to a rare breed of reporters who thrived on exclusives – journalists refer to them as scoops – which you hardly find today in our newsrooms. He cultivated his sources and they trusted him. His scoop days came to end when late one night, the feared midnight knock on the door came. Corrupt Practices Investigation Bureau (CPIB) officers went to his home and took him away. He and his wife were terrified. Suresh was interrogated for many hours: the officers wanted to know if he had bribed Central Narcotics Bureau officers to get his stories. Suresh denied the allegations. The episode had the effect the government intended, with Suresh wanting to move out of crime reporting and into sports journalism. I raised this with Minister George Yeo during a lunch meeting with editors. His cryptic reply: "Let the CPIB do its job." I muttered: "It is unlikely they will find anything." Nothing was found and Suresh did not hear further from the CPIB, but it achieved the chill effect the government wanted to send to Suresh and others who dared to tread its path.

Then came the General Election in 1997. Buried in the ashes of that bruising electoral battle was a story in *The New Paper* (TNP) which produced in full the police reports that a Workers' Party politician had made against Lee Kuan Yew and ten other PAP politicians on Polling Day. The day before, Opposition politician JB Jeyaretnam had uttered at an election rally on 1 January: "Finally, Mr Tang Liang Hong has just placed before me two reports he has made to the police against, you know, Mr Goh Chok Tong and his team."

In those police reports, it was alleged a number of PAP ministers had called Tang Liang Hong an anti-English educated, anti-Christian Chinese chauvinist, claims "likely to incite religious extremists to hate me and my family and cause harm to me and my family". Tang Liang Hong, a lawyer and Workers' Party candidate for the Cheng San Group Representation Constituency (GRC), was fighting an election for the first time. Although a rookie politician, he was regarded as a triple threat by the ruling party. Fluent and persuasive in Chinese, English and Malay, he marshalled his arguments forcefully and pushed PAP leaders to go on a verbal rampage, hurling accusation after accusation at him. The 1997 election campaign turned out to be one of the most toxic in recent history, with the PAP intent on preventing Tang Liang Hong and JBJ from getting into Parliament via the contest in Cheng San GRC.

I remember that rally speech by JBJ so well. He was the last speaker. He had finished his speech and was about to leave the stage when he was handed a piece of paper. He turned back to face the crowd of about 20,000 and uttered those fateful 28 words about the police reports. Technically, there was a case to sue JBJ as one would not make a police report to praise another person. So Lee Kuan Yew must have known that he had JBJ and Tang Liang Hong in his crosshairs. Don't forget that JBJ was the man who broke PAP's monopoly in Parliament when he took Anson in a by-election in 1981.

The next morning, just after I had put the polling day edition of TNP to bed and was enjoying a cup of coffee in the office canteen, my editor-in-chief called. "Get copies of the police reports from the Central Police Station and use them," said Cheong Yip Seng, a man of few words. "But the police don't release such reports to the media," I replied. "Call them. They will release them to you," came the immediate reply.

Word was sent to the printing department to stop the presses, and to the staff to wait for a new Page One lead. The buzz in the newsroom was palpable. I was excited as I knew this would be an exclusive for TNP. I was completely focused on speed, not on taking a step back and reflecting on the implications. As expected, the police refused to release the reports. When I told Cheong, he said he would get back to me. Within minutes, he was back on the line. "The reports will be faxed to you. You can see those to write your story," he said, matter of factly. The fax came and TNP celebrated its Page One scoop. To a journalist, nothing beats the adrenaline rush of landing a scoop and putting it together on a tight deadline, with printing and production colleagues hovering over one's shoulder. All the other papers used similar stories the next day.

The 11 PAP politicians took Tang Liang Hong and JBJ to court and accused them of libel. They wanted $12.9 million in "exemplary and aggravated" damages from Tang, for what they said were lies in his police report. The judge reduced those to $8.075 million and $3.63 million on appeal. The Opposition politician fled the country and has not returned since. How the media got hold of the police reports was raised in court by Tang's Queen's Counsel (QC), Charles Gray, when he said they were released by Lee Kuan Yew and Prime Minister Goh Chok Tong. They were playing politics, the QC said. "If the judge had known the facts concerning the police reports, he could and certainly should sharply have reduced the level of damages," the lawyer said.

In its appeal judgement, the court hearing the case said the PAP lawyers had said that Goh Chok Tong and Lee Kuan Yew released the police reports to the media. The judges said:[5]

> They [PAP lawyers] would have offered the court all the relevant facts, but it did not occur to them at the time, as the matter was never raised. We accept their explanation. It is quite clear that the oversight was not intentional.

The judges also addressed the point of why the two PAP leaders released the reports:[6]

> It seems to us that it was a matter of political exigency to the PAP leaders that the reports should be made public to neutralise whatever effect Tang sought to make out of them so that the voters could make their choice based on an informed basis.

Goh Chok Tong got $100,00 in damages from JBJ. The cases by the remaining PAP politicians were dropped and damages and costs waived, after JBJ apologised.

---

[5] *Tang Liang Hong v Lee Kuan Yew* [1997] 3 SLR(R) 576 at [183].
[6] *Tang Liang Hong v Lee Kuan Yew* [1997] 3 SLR(R) 576 at [180].

Before all this, and as the cases were coming up in court, I consulted a lawyer friend to find out the options open to me if a court ordered me to reveal the reporter's source. We agreed that I could not reveal the name as that would contravene a cardinal principle of journalism ethics. In the worst-case scenario, refusal to reveal the source would land me in court to face a charge of contempt of court. That did not happen, and another dance on the tightrope ended without a fall.

Six years earlier, in the aftermath of the 1991 General Election, the PAP under the new Prime Minister, Goh Chok Tong, had lost three seats to the Opposition, something that had hitherto seemed unthinkable in an overwhelmingly one-party Singapore. Realising the significance and news value of the event, TNP did the unthinkable in a country that was rather muted when it came to reporting on such political developments. Newspapers displaying even a semblance of anti-PAP sentiment or pro-Opposition views had a rough time with the establishment. Despite the possible political fallout, TNP sent reporters to the three Opposition-held constituencies – Hougang, Bukit Gombak and Nee Soon – and also to Buona Vista, where the ruling party had won big, with one clear direction: ask voters of these constituencies why they voted the way they did; note everything they say, do not self-censor, leave it to the editor to edit. The result was seven pages of pointed and sensational revelations with the headline "Why?" pulled through every page.

The reports documented the voters' dissatisfaction with PAP MPs who appeared to be strangers to their constituents. They were not out there meeting residents, listening to their problems or even connecting with them. One Hougang voter, Madam Isnahwati Harun, was quoted as saying: "Part of the problem is that Mr Tang (Tang Guan Seng, the defeated PAP candidate) didn't come across as the friendly type. He doesn't appear to be approachable. I have never met him before." James Lee said of his Bukit Batok MP, Seet Ai Mee: "When I met her at the meet-the-people session, she gave me such a cold look." On the other hand, the PAP candidate who scored the biggest boost in votes, Peter Sung, was popular with many residents of Buona Vista. "Some used the lift as a dustbin. After I told him about it, the problem was attended to immediately." Voters' unvarnished views were plastered in the different pages of the paper's post-election coverage.

The man who masterminded the coverage, Ken Jalleh Jr, said: "The decision to hit the ground running with the 'Why?' question was as pivotal as it was typical. Being popular was far from enough; we wanted to feel, reflect and be part of the pulse of the people. The 'Why?' approach was typical of TNP because the simplicity of the single-syllable question belied the complexity of the issue. It was in essence TNP's style of angle-shooting. It was instinctive." This type of grassroots reporting on the elections was unprecedented.

Every political journalist and editor becomes hypersensitive when it comes to election reporting, with editors scrutinising reporters' copy with an eagle eye. Those who tried to demonstrate some form of independence and fairness in their reporting and editing have paid a high price. *The Straits Times* editor, Han Fook Kwang, was sidelined and made managing editor after a rare display of fairness in political journalism when he gave the Opposition, especially the Workers' Party, more editorial space than what was allocated during previous elections. One example that will be remembered for a long time was *The Straits*

Times' Page One on the start of campaigning on 29 April 2011. It showed a big close-up picture of Deputy Prime Minister Teo Chee Hean walking up to the stage at the PAP's first rally in Pasir Ris-Punggol GRC, and below it, two smaller photos. One was of a Singapore Democratic Party rally; the other, of the humongous crowd at the Workers' Party rally in Hougang. It was that third picture that stunned Singapore. Pictures of election rallies, especially high-angled shots, are a minefield because the Opposition rallies attract many more people than those held by PAP politicians. The PAP's fear was that such pictures would raise the political temperature and spur more people to vote for the Opposition. The herd instinct, if you want to call it. The ruling party appeared to regard elections as something of an irritation, a statutory nuisance that should be gotten over with quickly and surgically. Restrictions such as limiting election campaigning to nine days were introduced to curb the excitement factor. However, the advent of social media in 2006 and its free-wheeling coverage of election rallies exerted heavy pressure on the mainstream media such as *The Straits Times*, which was beginning to feel the pinch and pain of its declining readership and had to rethink its election coverage. Since Singaporeans had something to compare with *The Straits Times*' coverage (i.e., online media), the chorus against the newspaper grew and put pressure on editors like Han Fook Kwang to find a new way, but his removal as ST editor stopped the process of change in its tracks.

TNP's "Why?" coverage surprised some observers, with one even saying that I might get into trouble. Another said TNP was brave to do this kind of reporting. As we worked on the reports, I was clear about one thing: TNP would not continue to pursue this angle as that might give the government a reason to scrutinise our intentions. Past experience had shown that in similar situations, it would want to see if there was a trend in coverage and ask their well-known question: what is their agenda? The newsroom was told this was a one-hit wonder and there would be no other similar reports, analyses and commentaries, but the unexpected happened: the Chinese-language press, noting that TNP was not taken to task, went to town with reports on the PAP candidates who lost. *The Straits Times* also jumped in.

The 1991 election result was a personal and political blow for Goh Chok Tong, who was leading the party in his first general election as Prime Minister. His strategy of putting himself as the election issue, saying he was seeking a clear signal from voters for a more open and consultative style of government, backfired. Then came the inevitable call from the Istana to editors. At the meeting with editors, Goh Chok Tong put his Mr Nice Guy image aside and lectured us to stop such reporting. I remember how he looked at me sternly when he said: "You attack him. I will make him my Political Secretary." The man he meant was Tang Guan Seng, who had been the incumbent MP for Hougang. His constituents had criticised him for being an absentee MP. Elected in 1988, he was defeated after one term by Low Thia Khiang of the Workers' Party. Within days, Tang Guan Seng would be appointed as Political Secretary to the Prime Minister.

One thing that began to worry me was that fear was becoming pervasive in Singapore. Conversations would start openly enough but quickly become awkward when government personalities and policies were mentioned. Sometimes, when discussions became heated and loud, it was not unusual to see some looking behind them to check for eavesdroppers. I did not pay much attention to this trend until a lawyer friend called to say he wanted to discuss a private matter. He came to my home, but requested that we go for a walk. "Your home is not private enough. I am sure it is bugged," he said. That became the subject of a column I wrote for *The New Paper* in October 1999. I used that encounter to comment on Prime Minister Goh Chok Tong's appeal to Singaporeans to debate issues freely. How, I asked, would people debate freely if the fear factor hung over conversations that some deemed controversial? I concluded: "As long as the government is perceived as Big Brother waiting to pounce on those who are critical of policies, and as long as the talented and the bright imagine a conspiracy at every corner, you tell me, how to become a world-class country?"[7]

Soon after the column appeared, I got a call from the office of David Lim, then Minister of State (Information and the Arts), asking if I was free for lunch. I did not give it much thought as such lunches with political officeholders were nothing out of the ordinary. However, that particular lunch date has stayed with me. As the meal wore on, I realised the minister wanted to convince me that the fear issue was just a matter of perception. I disagreed. He caught me off guard with this question: "What would you do if your reporter comes to you with a story that a minister is corrupt?" I replied: "We will do all our checks and go to the PM for comment." And then what? he wanted to know. Depending on what the PM says, we will make a decision on publication. What he said next surprised me: "No, you should not publish it. Let the PM investigate and decide what to do."

---

[7] PN Balji, "4-letter word that bugs", *The New Paper*, 23 October 1999.

Without missing a beat, I asked: "What if the PM is also corrupt?" After an awkward silence, he said: "Then the country is finished."

Lunch ended and I walked away wondering what that was all about. Thirty years later, I am still puzzled. Was he trying to figure out where I stood on the question of national interest? Or was it to get my inner thoughts on the role of the press? Or what I thought about investigative journalism, a no-go area for the government? Perhaps there was no hidden agenda, but a young and rising political star trying to be useful to his colleagues and superiors in the Cabinet.

Encounters like this were an addition to the regular feature of officialdom's media policy of using fear, intimidation and the force of law to get the media to tell every nuance of the Government's side of the story and downplay dissenting views. From Lee Kuan Yew downwards, ministers discussed matters of state and answered questions with candour during these meetings. The meetings cut both ways. Editors knew they were in a charmed circle, being privy to the policymakers' thinking, but these off-the-record sessions were also a double-edged sword as they tied editors' hands. When reporters uncovered stories on which editors had already been briefed, such stories had to be held back until the official announcements were made. Editors also found themselves hemmed in when they evaluated stories, because they always had to bear in mind what had been discussed with the ministers. Such privileged meetings hung like an albatross around many editors' necks.

Some meetings did get tense and testy, especially one in 1991 when George Yeo, then Minister (Information and the Arts), and *The Straits Times* editor, Leslie Fong, crossed swords over a commentary by Sumiko Tan.

Sumiko had criticised NTUC deputy secretary general Goh Chee Wee after he made a "startling revelation" in Parliament that 12 per cent, or 156,000 of the workforce, earned less than $400 a month. Finance Minister Richard Hu countered that this group comprised mainly part-timers and students working on vacation. In her column, Sumiko said:[8]

> ... Did the Member know the profile of these low-wage workers when he cited the statistics? If he did, then he did the House a disservice by misleading members just to strengthen his argument – something one would not expect of a PAP MP. And if he did not, then it says a great deal about the amount of homework he had done before arguing his case ... As a union leader, one would assume that Mr Goh has enough research staff to back him up with facts and figures when he wants to argue a matter concerning workers. He cannot be excused for not having accurate information here. But if he or his staff had tried and could not get such relatively simple data, then all that talk of striving for a higher level of public discussion of important issues must just remain just that – talk.

Chay Wai Chuen defended his fellow PAP MP in a letter to *The Straits Times*: "In fairness to Goh Chee Wee, I would say that he made a substantially correct statement about the income profile of workers ... Mr Goh never said that the data he used was basically correct," he wrote.

Leslie Fong replied in a rejoinder:[9]

---

[8] Sumiko Tan, "Debate wrapped up in the usual brisk, unflappable style", *The Straits Times*, 13 March 1991, page 23.

[9] Leslie Fong, replying to a letter by Parliamentarian Chay Wai Chuen, "MP largely correct about income profile of workers", *The Straits Times*, 21 March 1991, page 30.

All (Sumiko) did was to ask two pointed questions and say what she would have thought of Mr Goh in one or the other situation. What influenced her was Mr Goh's failure to stand up to the Finance Minister there and then to defend his set of figures ... I would like to assure Mr Chay that our journalists do strive to be accurate and judicious in their reporting and commentary. Dare we hope that MPs, not exactly known to be reticent about what they think of the media, would do the same?

There were all the qualifiers, all the ifs and buts. Still, the sting of Sumiko's commentary and Leslie's defence was evident. This became the subject of another of George Yeo's regular meetings with editors. When the Goh Chee Wee affair came up, Yeo put forward the government view, and Leslie the newspaper's. When the discussion got intense, Yeo said: "Our MPs may be wrong but the Government will protect them at all costs." Coming from a minister many regarded as a rare progressive voice in the political establishment, it was a surprise. Leslie replied: "Yes, minister. We know it will be our blood on the floor." An awkward silence hung over the dining room. The minister stood up, smiled, shook hands and left. We knew that a new line had been drawn and a new out-of-bounds marker set.

That same year, 1991, *The New Paper* got into a flap with MP Davinder Singh, a well-known litigator. In Parliament, Davinder criticised the "less-than-serious coverage" of the first Gulf War by a newspaper. He didn't name the newspaper. Later, when asked by *The Straits Times* to name the paper, he pointed the finger at *The New Paper*. It came as a surprise to us in the newsroom as our coverage had been well received and appreciated by many. As editor, I thought our journalists and our readers deserved a more complete explanation and specifics of what he meant. I sent Davinder 36 issues of TNP's war coverage, asking him to pinpoint the areas he found wanting. Then, TNP writer Irene Hoe and I met him in his office. Davinder picked out four articles he found objectionable. They included a Page One report with a headline that screamed "Save Saddam". Another had a Hitleresque caricature of then Iraqi president Saddam Hussein pumping oil into the Persian Gulf in a comic-style satirical representation.

In essence, Davinder thought TNP was trivialising a serious issue. He was especially critical of the comic-style illustration. He told us: "This is not the war. This is frivolous. I am saying you can't lighten the war. I am saying there is a line beyond which you should not go, when you ascribe reasons which are totally frivolous when the people involved are totally serious." My response: "The comic strips appeared in a column called 'Fowl Play Chicks'. On top of the column, its purpose was made clear – to take a wacky look at people, shows and issues in the news." On the portrayal of Saddam as Hitler, Davinder said: "To portray him in this light was a little light. Immediately I got the impression: good grief, it could have been more serious. Once you turn the page, to be absolutely fair, you are accurate in your coverage." I accepted his point and said that the coverage went very close to the line. Finally, I asked Davinder: "When you talk to your constituents in Toa Payoh and when you address Parliament, do you use the same language? TNP is trying to talk to the residents in your constituency." The matter ended amicably and Davinder and I became good friends after that encounter.

Three years later, in 1994, I had to deal with another TNP critic. This time, it was a government bigwig – Minister in the Prime Minister's Office and NTUC Secretary General, Lim Boon Heng. In a commentary in *NTUC News*, he ticked off *Shin Min*

Daily News and *Lianhe Wanbao*, and in the process took a swipe at TNP. "While I admire the way *The New Paper* sometimes presents complex issues in simple form, I am dismayed when it sinks to the gutter with sexually explicit stories," he wrote, in a commentary headlined "Money And Values". His bigger point was that newspapers should avoid "exploiting yellow culture" to pump up circulation. "The bottom line is important. But equally important is the need to preserve our value system," he concluded.[10] His complaint gave me an opportunity to talk about how TNP had morphed into a new product since its launch six years earlier. I published Lim's commentary in full and wrote a response:[11]

> The old TNP has been the subject of a lot of introspection by the senior editorial team over the last one year ... The result is a new TNP which readers see before them. It is the culmination of a number of strategic changes to our editorial philosophy without sacrificing our vibrancy ... Yes, we want to make money. No, the profit motive does not soar above our mission statement to inform, educate and entertain.

Lim's PR minder, Ee Boon Lee, called me soon after the report was published. He said: "Tuan, very good response. I am sending you a bottle of Chivas Regal." That bottle never came.

---

[10] Lim Boon Heng, "Money And Values", reproduced in *The New Paper*, 17 August 1994, page 10.
[11] PN Balji, replying to Lim Boon Heng's commentary "Money And Values" in *The New Paper*, 17 August 1994, page 10.

CHAPTER 4

The Misunderstood Paper
What a foreign editor saw that others did not

It took the perceptive eye of a senior British newspaperman to dissect *The New Paper* and detect its soul, a soul hidden by the in-your-face headlines and bare-it-all pictures splashed on its front pages. Peter Preston's words went against the popular narrative: "*The New Paper* is a friend, taking your hand in a difficult world and helping you make sense of it," he wrote in *The Observer* newspaper in 1998. The veteran journalist said:[1]

> Explanation is the key. Questions, answers. It's bouncy and never boring, often written through the eyes of the readers themselves. Pre-Budget coverage included an open letter to a soap star on honeymoon, telling her how to get her finances organised. The ingenuity is constant, and so thinly disguised is the educative purpose.

He was in the audience when I gave a presentation on *The New Paper* at an editors' conference in Penang. He seemed intrigued, did some research and wrote not just a flattering article but one that went to the heart of the paper's editorial mission.

---

[1] Peter Preston, "The New Paper success", a reprint of *The Observer*'s article in *The Straits Times*, 26 November 1998.

He even recommended that Britain's Labour Party, the political organisation that Prime Minister Tony Blair tried to remake as New Labour, should take a leaf from *The New Paper*'s book. Preston said in his article:

> New Labour is awash with young voters trying to make more for themselves, toiling all hours, inured to cynicism. Hundreds of thousands of them need and want a hand ... What's Dr Mahathir Mohamad up to? What is this $7-billion hole in the Singapore Budget? Why have Asian economies caught a cold and what does it mean for me? The responses are a model of practical clarity. They have a mission to explain.

On its home turf, however, *The New Paper* (TNP) was "The Misunderstood Paper". It was seen very differently by many who fired missiles at the team. In 1994, NTUC Secretary General Lim Boon Heng, who was concurrently Minister in the Prime Minister's Office, wrote in a commentary in the labour organisation's newsletter in 1994: "While I admire the way *The New Paper* sometimes explains complex issues in simple form, I am dismayed when it sinks to the gutter with sexually explicit stories."[2]

The unkindest cut came from within. We found out that the wife of a senior editor of TNP had ordered him not to take the paper home. "This is not a family paper," she was believed to have told him. Another story is that of a venerable Ministry of Foreign Affairs official who protested to one of TNP's founding editors, Irene Hoe, when she showed up at a conference: "Your

---

[2] Lim Boon Heng, "Money and Values", reproduced in *The New Paper*, 17 August 1994, page 10.

newspaper is so sensational!" Already primed and ready for such barbs, she responded with a smile of delight and this rejoinder: "Why, thank you! We do think it is pretty sensational!"

There were also the enthusiasts who were unafraid to declare that they read and enjoyed TNP, notably the Senior Minister of State for Education, Dr Tay Eng Soon. In 1990, the Vocational and Industrial Training Board (VITB) hosted a meet-the-press lunch. A gilt-edged opportunity, we thought, to market our newspaper as a vehicle for VITB's recruitment and other advertising. Representing TNP at this event was Irene Hoe, by now a seasoned hand at representing the paper. She recalls that she lay in wait at the doorway with copies of the day's paper under her arm, hot off the press. As Dr Tay, the board's chairman, walked in, she held out a paper and said: "Brought you the latest news." The first Gulf War was then at its height and to her delight, Dr Tay immediately opened the paper and began reading. A minute or so later, he blushed and apologised. "I am so sorry! But I just had to see what was going on in the Middle East! *The New Paper* always has the latest news on the Gulf War. I haven't been in my office at all today and I'm so used to having *The New Paper* waiting for me on my desk." Irene's smile of surprise widened into a full-out triumphant grin, as Dr Tay continued: "My son is a huge fan of *The New Paper*. He will call me to remind me to be sure to bring the paper home. He really likes the infographics and even files some away."

Dr Tay recognised and understood our mission, and appreciated the rigours of the balancing act our journalists had to perform: delivering a paper that readers would want to buy, and making it politically and socially relevant. And yes, educational. We settled on a roughly 80/20 blend; 80 per cent human interest content,

20 per cent coverage of political and foreign events in a way that readers appreciated and understood. Sometimes, when the planets were aligned, these fields converged, such as when the Tiananmen Square protests happened in Beijing in May to June 1989.

Reporters Melvin Singh and Irene Ng were trailblazers in providing the serious news for the paper. Irene took care of political coverage, while Melvin made his name by parachuting into countries that were plunged into one crisis after another.

Melvin arrived at TNP when Southeast Asia seemed to be teetering on the brink of economic and political apocalypse. The Asian financial contagion was spreading from Thailand to Malaysia to Indonesia. The very core of their political systems was under attack. Riots in mid-1998 brought Indonesia under President Suharto to a tipping point. The strongman was tottering and Melvin was there to report the drama and analyse the consequences. He recollected: "I was fortunate that I had five years' experience in the police force, working as an investigating officer and drug detective. I knew which areas to avoid and which places were safe to operate in. My working knowledge of Malay also helped."

The Indonesian government was in a state of paralysis with university students rioting, burning and looting property. They were baying for Suharto's blood. "Photographer Mohd Ishak and I were in the middle of all this. Once a bomb went off very close to where we were standing. Ishak was adamant in getting a photograph, he turned back, took a shot and we ran to take cover," said Melvin.

There were other scary moments. Mohd Ishak described one that took place when he went to report the fall of another strongman, Saddam Hussein, in 2003:

Reporter Azhar Ghani and I had just crossed Iraq's border with Jordan when a gun-toting man in army attire told the driver of our jeep to stop. There were two stark choices in front of us. Stop and risk being shot dead or speed off and pray for that slim chance of survival. We took the latter route, the gunman was taken by surprise and by the time he got his composure back, we had moved on. He still shot at us, we ducked and didn't dare to raise our heads until we were a safe distance away. That was when reality hit us. The back window of the jeep was riddled with bullets; we were lucky to be alive.

Both Irene and Melvin were raw reporters who had just a few years' experience in the subjects they were covering. They had the basic reporting skills and instincts, were enterprising and eager to jump into the deep end of the pool and learn to swim. Irene went one step further, using the opportunity not only to report but also to make the career leap from political journalist to politician. After a successful stint with TNP, she earned an MSc at the London School of Economics, then moved to *The Straits Times*. It provided a more prominent platform which became the launch pad for her political career with the ruling party as a Member of Parliament. TNP also benefited from her political contacts. Her interviews with Lee Kuan Yew and Lee Hsien Loong raised the paper's profile in the eyes of decision makers and serious-minded readers. One of her more memorable interviews was with Lee Hsien Loong, then Deputy Prime Minister, after he was diagnosed with lymphoma in 1992 and had just started on 18 weeks of chemotherapy. Irene recalled:

> The Deputy Prime Minister was bald. Tubes stuck out from a dressing over his chest. Because of his compromised immune system, doctors

advised him to stay away from crowds. That he would make time for an interview to instil public confidence in the Government said much about … his trust in me and TNP.

Then there was the interview with Dr Tay Eng Soon, the Senior Minister of State for Education, in April 1993. Recalling that interview, Irene said: "For the first time, he revealed that he had battled five illnesses in his lifetime." He had cancer, diabetes, heart and eye diseases and a skin condition. He asked that we delay publishing the interview as he was worried about the timing, given DPM Lee Hsien Loong's condition. Irene remembered:

> We withheld the story. Sadly, Dr Tay passed away on August 5 from a heart attack. We published the interview the next day, and some of his own Cabinet colleagues told me later that they had not known that Dr Tay had been through so much and sacrificed so much for the country.

Irene's interviews gave us the much-needed armour to blunt the many knives constantly aimed at TNP. In reporting on serious issues, however, the paper never deviated from its bold presentation. The 1992 interview with DPM Lee Hsien Loong had just three words in the headline: "Cancer And I". It was accompanied by a rarity, a stark picture of him bald-headed and looking vulnerable, staring back at you. It reminded readers of how fragile life could be, and how unfortunate and unpredictable events could unsettle Singapore's political succession, however meticulously planned it had been. It was a precarious time in Singapore politics as the other DPM, Ong Teng Cheong, was also unexpectedly diagnosed with cancer at about the same time, leaving a big question mark over the future leadership as DPM Lee Hsien Loong was widely expected to become Singapore's third prime minister.

For many editors, it was the ashen-faced father of a cancer patient that refused to go away. As he walked into the meeting room at the Istana to brief them about his son's illness, the toll on his face showed. It was not the face of the Lee Kuan Yew they had seen often, the strong and forthright leader who never allowed emotions to interfere with his iron will to get his country going, but he composed himself to tell us what we wanted to know about his son's illness. Indeed, it seemed that with his usual thoroughness, he had done enough research to write a minor thesis on his son's cancer.

My favourite story of a politician in TNP was that of a founding member of the People's Action Party, Othman Wok, who had once been Minister for Social Affairs. In September 1998, at a party to celebrate Lee Kuan Yew's 75th birthday, the former prime minister and then senior minister gave a glowing tribute to Othman Wok. As Lee recalled his comrade-in-arms' unshakeable loyalty and the critical role he had played in supporting him in the face of attacks by Malaysia's ruling Malay extremists in the 1960s, emotions gave way to tears. Reporter Ng Wan Ching captured the moment in her report:

> The mood was pleasant and the birthday boy was in good spirits, mingling with his old comrades who had fought with him to make Singapore happen. Then the unexpected happened. Mid-way through his speech, the Senior Minister broke down. Tears in his eyes, licking his lips, his voice breaking down ... the big screens in the Suntec City ballroom captured Mr Lee's emotions up close for

the 1,200 guests. There was hardly any movement, any noise, in the ballroom. Many eyes were fixed on the big screens. Some just did not want to see.

Othman Wok was the man of the moment. The day after the event, TNP decided to send a young reporter, Yong Siew Fern, to interview him. The editors told her something unthinkable at that time: just go and talk to him about everything and anything. Go with an open mind. Don't read anything about him. The editors believed that if she went fully prepared with what had been reported earlier, she would turn in a predictably dull story. Going totally unprepared, they thought, would lead her to discover fresh angles. Doing research on the person you were going to interview was accepted newsroom practice which TNP decided to turn on its head. The strategy worked. The former minister, always a gregarious character, opened up and revealed several surprising gems of hitherto private information about himself on such topics as his second marriage and his circumcision. In *The Straits Times* newsroom, Richard Lim was so taken with Siew Fern's interview that he published it in full in *The Sunday Times* the next day.

Wok had gotten married a second time, to a Singaporean in Thailand in 1976. It was done in secret, but, somehow, Lee Kuan Yew came to know of it. Siew Fern's report said:[3]

> He called me and said: "Is it true?" I said: "Yes." "So why did you do it," he asked. I said I was unhappy. Then he said: "Go to Indonesia."

---

[3] Yong Siew Fern, "Surprise, surprise, he's so funny", *The Sunday Times*, 26 September 1998, page 18.

But if I couldn't solve my personal problem, he suggested I could not continue my work. So I went to Indonesia in 1977. I didn't solve my problem. In 1980, I retired (at 56).

Of the circumcision, Wok said:

> The knife was like a steak knife. I sat on the edge of the chair with a tray of ashes in front of my feet to catch the blood. Some relatives came to hold me down. Then I heard a 'whoop'. I looked down and didn't see anything. I thought the whole thing must have gone. After that they bandaged it, and wah, the pain …

TNP made an art of "telling it differently". Tamal Mukherjee, the pioneer TNP journalist from India, was involved in one effort when the world was going through tumultuous times. The Soviet Union had collapsed, Iraq had overrun its tiny neighbour, Kuwait, and George Bush Sr had assembled a coalition to drive out Iraqi forces from Kuwait, an event that is remembered as the First Gulf War. Tamal said:

> I did a number of centrespread features to explain the issues behind the turmoil. One was on the Stealth bomber. Nobody had heard of or seen the Stealth bomber that was used in the US attacks. We were lucky to have with us the father of newspaper graphics, Peter Sullivan. We worked on that feature for a month. Peter and I visited many toy shops to look at toy models of fighter aircraft.

TNP's coverage of the Gulf War was a breakthrough moment in the sun. Under the supervision of foreign editor Rosnah Ahmad, the paper went to town with breaking news and more. Much of the military action happened after dark in the Gulf, when *The Straits Times* had gone to bed, but well within TNP's deadline. The "more" came from backgrounding, explanations, and TNP's intensive and realistic imaginative and often unexpected use of graphics and illustrations. When Saddam made one of his madman threats to dump petrol into the Persian Gulf, illustrator Hup Lee, better known as Hup, drew a caricature of a modern-day Hitler holding a pump and pouring oil into the sea. Hup Lee said: "I wanted to show his treachery and brutality in graphic form. I could not think of another person other than the murderous Hitler to get across that point."

The result: daily circulation exploded from about 50,000 copies a day to between 100,000 and 150,000, even on occasions breaching the 200,000 mark. Rosnah and her small team took the stories that came from the news agencies and reworked them into words and images that made the events relevant to our readers. News agencies write for a global audience, not for our readers. The idea was to take that material and turn it into stories and visuals to show readers the significance of these momentous events to a small country like Singapore and its multi-ethnic population that was beginning to feel the strains of economic, religious and racial pulls. To some in the Malay community, Saddam Hussein appeared heroic for standing up to the Big Bad West. To some, that lionisation was troubling. To others, including Member of Parliament Davinder Singh, it was TNP's bold explanatory graphics that were troubling. He thought they were over the top and said as much in Parliament. While he and some others may have found those graphics discomfiting, they did the important job of examining the underlying issues for readers.

TNP journalists were always on a relentless pursuit to do things differently. Stories had to have a twist, pages had to be designed with the "wow" factor in mind, photographs had to have an unexpected angle, an unexpected touch. Day in, day out, the journalists were on a treadmill that refused to stop.

When a major earthquake hit Taiwan in September 1999, the team decided to cover it ... well ... differently. Instead of dispatching a team immediately, reporter Tanya Fong and photographer Simon Ker were sent there two months later in November. Nearly all the journalists who had rushed to cover the story had already left, hunting for the next "flavour" to report on.

The instruction to the TNP team was simple: bring back stories and pictures of a nation that was recovering and rebuilding. They came back with a report and picture of a building that was tilted 45 degrees. "We went in to see for ourselves what it was like being in there. To move up and down the tilted building, we used a rope to get our balance right," said photographer Simon. Fear of another earthquake happening had gripped the people. "We saw people staying in tents that they had set up outside their homes," he said.

Water is an existential issue in Singapore. It is used to drum into the national psyche the security and economic consequences of a squeeze on the water supply. Artist Hup Lee used cartoons to convey its impact on the populace, creating an imaginary Singaporean household to capture a dire and imaginary situation of the day when the taps ran dry. Twenty-six years later, a creative team led by Ken Jalleh Jr applied the same device, updating it to convey to the people in Singapore the urgency for a two-stage 30 per cent hike in the price of water. The headline for both pieces of work was the same, it was conversational and relatable: "How Come No Water?"

The world can change, artificial intelligence may complicate things, disruptions may overhaul companies ... but TNP's approach to communicating with readers will remain evergreen.

CHAPTER 5

Toh Chin Chye Affair
A footloose newsroom culture gone wrong

The New Paper is an oddball in Singapore journalism. No other newspaper in the country had ever attempted the journalistic curveballs that this idiosyncratic newcomer lobbed at its audience, and Singapore is unlikely to see another like it. From the start, *The New Paper* was irreverent, brash, sometimes even fearless – all qualities that made it a misfit in an orderly and straight-jacketed Singapore. Like so many things in this country, it would not have been born – much less survived – if not for the government. It was the offspring of the government's desire for a newspaper that would meet one of its political objectives: to speak the language of blue-collar workers. These were readers who found *The Straits Times* too heavy in both language and content.

This was Lee Kuan Yew's idea. He wanted an English-language newspaper that mirrored the Chinese-language *Shin Min Daily News*. Although he did not articulate it publicly in so many words, shrewd politician that he was, he realised that many of his government's politics and policies went effectively above the heads of those whose understanding of written English was at best perfunctory and that they might easily be swayed to vote against the political party of which he was a founder. This belief ran counter to his ambition to have every gap covered, every information vacuum filled. Nothing should be left to chance. From womb to tomb, the People's Action Party should be omnipresent and omnipotent in the country.

The New Paper took this as tacit approval to introduce a kind of journalism never before seen in Singapore. Doing it differently became the mantra of the newspaper. Doing it differently meant doggedly tracking down exclusives, striving to give a creative twist to a story, pushing barriers to craft headlines that grabbed readers by the jugular, hunting for that refreshing subject or an unexpected photograph of a mundane event, challenging artists to design a WOW! page. Such a newspaper needed a newsroom that enabled an anarchic artistry to flourish. That approach also had its downside. Let the staff loose and you might well have a crisis on your hands. On the flipside, tight control would lead to a paper that was dull and boring.

Into this newsroom sauntered Yaw Yan Chong, a crime reporter from *The Straits Times* who knew that *The New Paper*, with its unconventional approach to news, would be his happy hunting ground. The newsroom he had come from was staid and predictable, used to following rules to a T, and in a way, it had to be because of its traditions and a history dating back to 1845. In fact, as one newsroom wit had put it, *The Straits Times* is a Singapore heritage that should come under the Preservation of Monuments Board! A free spirit such as Yan Chong was a misfit there but an ideal hire for *The New Paper*, which thrived on his willingness and ability to roam the streets, eavesdrop on conversations and drink with his police buddies.

To survive in such a culture of organised chaos, one had to have a sensitive antenna and learn to hone the ability to read the political tea leaves. That person also needed the innate skill to know which barriers could not be crossed, and which were the strictures that could be compromised.

As you entered the newsroom, the first thing you would see was the coffee machine. This was artist Hup Lee's favourite tool for making the staff laugh at themselves. No one was spared. From editor to office girl and boy, no one was sacrosanct. His wicked doodles tore into the newsroom's personalities. Hup said:

> I started doodling Mala, our newsroom office girl. She was our mascot, our little Girl Friday. Those doodles were a hit, with people even making photocopies of her caricatures. That gave me the motivation to experiment further. I did one of the editor sitting in Mala's chair. There was no comeback and I never looked back.

The diminutive Mala with her infectious grin and trademark pigtails was regularly caricatured going through the pages of *The New Paper*. She was also given the task of looking at the Page One design before it was sent to the production department. Her brief was simple: tell us if you understand the Page One lead headline. If she didn't, many of our readers wouldn't, and the headline had to be changed. She was special and she knew it. This was all part of doing it differently.

This free-spirited culture was shattered on 20 January 1996, when a sensational story by Yan Chong screamed from Page One: "Ex-DPM Toh Chin Chye Arrested".

The accompanying story said: "Former DPM Toh Chin Chye was arrested in connection with a hit-and-run accident in which a 17-year-old student was killed. The founding chairman of the

PAP was arrested last Thursday. He was released after bail of $10,000 was put up, sources said." Other details: Dr Toh was driving a red Toyota van. Police traced the vehicle to a public housing car park in Tampines. The van driver was drunk.

A former deputy prime minister driving a pick-up? The vehicle parked in an HDB car park? He was drunk? The holes in the report were so obvious that, looking at them 13 years later, it was surprising that nobody raised the alarm.

Having lived and breathed *The New Paper* for a dozen years and having replayed that calamitous embarrassment in my mind many, many times, I have an explanation. It was a calamity waiting to happen. When the thrill of getting an exclusive overtakes everything else, disasters happen. Sometimes even obvious minefields are ignored or explained away. The Big Desk editor who was at the centre of it all, Ken Jalleh Jr, listed three other factors that led to the fiasco.

Wrong Assumption: Yan Chong was the paper's undisputed star journalist, a crime reporter with solid police sources. He was the envy of his peers for his series of stories on rogue cops, reports that had annoyed the police establishment. He trusted the traffic sergeant who had given him the lead. When asked if it was the former DPM, the source confirmed that he knew who Toh Chin Chye was. In the end, it turned out that the driver in the report was another Toh Chin Chye, not the former top politician.

Many years later, I spoke about this episode to the man whose duty it was to give the green light to send the paper to press. Had he, I asked, noticed the glaring flaws in the story? That man, Ng Whay Hock, who has an ironclad reputation for spotting holes from miles away, said:

I was talking to one of the sub-editors about the story. I told him that it couldn't be the former DPM, it must be another Toh Chin Chye. I spoke to the reporter. But he insisted his source was correct. I checked the phone directory and found nine Toh Chin Chyes. Then fate intervened. The Prime Minister's Office called to say they were sending us a press release. The caller did not say what it was about and I didn't ask as I was more interested to organise the newsroom and the production people so that the paper might be delayed with the late-breaking story coming from PMO. Something told me that the government was reacting to the Toh Chin Chye story.

In fact, the statement from the Prime Minister's Office was about Mr Lee Kuan Yew being admitted to hospital with chest pains.

Fatal Distraction: the PMO statement sent the newsroom into a frenzy to accommodate the breaking news on Page One. In the rush and excitement, the editors were distracted and the Toh Chin Chye story did not get the attention it would otherwise have had from other pairs of eyes. It was like a perfect storm waiting to happen.

Procedural Deviation: The story was omitted from the daily schedule, a copy of which always went to the editor-in-chief. This omission went against standard operating procedure. Had the editor-in-chief been in the loop and seen that storyline on the schedule, he would have asked: "Are you sure?" The reporter and Ken Jalleh were so consumed with breaking the story and so confident of the source's credentials, that they were prepared to go ahead without verifying the story with other sources. Even a call to the official police spokesman was not made, as they feared that the police might intervene to hush up the story or even send a press release to all media.

When the paper hit the streets, top Singapore Press Holdings (SPH) executives and government officials immediately deluged the newsroom with calls. Shocked journalists attempted damage control. Circulation and other staff rushed out to retrieve unsold copies. Three apologies, including one in *The Straits Times*, were published, but the damage was done. Dr Toh Chin Chye demanded hefty compensation – eventually reduced to $300,000 through the intercession of his former comrade-in-arms, Mr Lim Kim San, then executive chairman of SPH.

While all this was happening, I was away in India. I had just completed a pilgrimage to a mountain temple in Kerala, southern India. I was inundated with calls to my father-in-law's home. Ivan Fernandez, the acting editor of *The New Paper*, was profoundly and abjectly apologetic. Editor-in-chief Cheong Yip Seng was worried about morale in the newsroom. A friend who called was scathing in his condemnation and said this was the biggest sin in Singapore journalism. I decided to fly back immediately. In those days, there were no direct flights between Kerala and Singapore. I would have to fly to Chennai in Tamil Nadu, and onward to Singapore. But that day, there were no flights leaving Calicut, where I was, for Chennai. So I had to take a circuitous route, first north to Bombay, then south to Chennai. When I went to the Singapore Airlines office in Chennai, I was told the flight was fully booked. Try Malaysian Airlines, the kind staff told me. The counter officer at the MAS office was intrigued about the urgency to rush home. I told her about the crisis at work and she said: "Yah, we are all talking about it." Luckily, I managed to get a ticket, but only to Kuala Lumpur, as MAS didn't fly direct from Chennai to Singapore. Finally, I arrived in Singapore from Kuala Lumpur, anxious, worried and exhausted.

The first call I got after I landed was from Yan Chong. "Boss, you were so right. You told me the night before you left for your pilgrimage that if I continue to cut corners, one day I might get into big trouble," he said, showing no outward sign of the crisis engulfing him and our newspaper. It was like one of the chats I would have with him about work, life and anything under the sun. He was a likeable chap, very obliging and down to earth. The night before I left Singapore, I had told him:

> Yan Chong, I was a crime reporter once. When I see the line in your story that says "an eyewitness who declined to be named", I suspect there is no such person. What if the police tell you they want to talk to the eyewitness to get more information, will you decline to give them the name? If you decline, then they can accuse you of being a hindrance to their investigation. Please think about it.

I regret not having been firmer with him. If I had, maybe, just maybe, we would not have gotten into that mess. The newsroom I walked into on my return from India resembled a morgue. The lively fun atmosphere was gone. Even the burbling coffee machine had fallen silent. Everyone was looking behind his back. A deathly hush hung over the newsroom. Newsroom staffers stared blankly at their computer terminals, fearful of what might come next.

An inquiry panel under *Business Times* editor, Patrick Daniel, was set up to look into what had led to the publication of the story and to see if acting editor Ivan Fernandez, Big Desk editor

Ken Jalleh Jr and reporter Yaw Yan Chong were negligent. The panel found all three negligent. It concluded:

> Although none of the offences involved any moral turpitude, appropriate severe disciplinary action is called for in view of the gravity of the damage caused. Apart from the substantial damages that SPH will have to pay to Dr Toh, the error has also severely damaged TNP's credibility, SPH's image and the journalism profession here.

When the senior editors of SPH met, nearly all of them felt that all three involved should be given marching orders. I stayed silent right through the meeting. So did Cheong Yip Seng. The editor-in-chief's face was difficult to read. I decided to talk to him in private. I told him that sacking all three would be like committing *hara-kiri*. The paper, I said, would be pushed into a dark pit from which it might never be able to crawl out. Cheong listened. Then I suggested a compromise: let the reporter go and demote both the editors. I knew what the impact would be on the newsroom floor. There would be accusations that Management was protecting its own. This, I reasoned, would be the lesser of two evils.

Cheong listened without uttering a word. When the decision was made a few days later, my recommendation was accepted. Losing a journalist, especially a talent like Yan Chong, was devastating. Morale hit rock bottom, and that was an understatement. I had never seen the newsroom in that state. A reporter who joined three months after the debacle said: "The newsroom was subdued. There was a sense that stricter reporting procedures were being introduced."

The tension, uncertainty and fear in the newsroom were made worse after it was announced that Bertha Henson, then a senior editor with *The Straits Times*, would shore up the editing team. She was a tough taskmaster not known to mince her words when presented with shoddy work. In characteristic Bertha fashion, she pronounced in an interview:

> *The New Paper* was a chaotic place with not enough disciplined editorial procedures. The front-end editors were not setting enough standards. The newsroom was as apprehensive to receive me as I was to go there. There was a sense that I was there to crack the whip, so to speak. And that I would bring ST's conservative and straight-laced values into the newsroom.

I gave my undivided attention to getting the journalists to return to what they had been before this unprecedented setback. What Cheong Yip Seng told me when I agreed to become editor in 1990, six years earlier, reverberated in my mind: "We are paying you this salary not for doing your day-to-day job. It is to take us out of a crisis quickly if we are to be hit by one."

I set about trying to do just that. The first thing I had to do was to find out if our readers were rejecting us. Would they be wondering if they could trust reports in our newspaper? At the time, fake news had not become the plague it is now, and social media was not even a figment in the imagination. Circulation figures were holding steady and there seemed hardly any negative reaction from the marketplace. That gave me the time and space to tackle the single biggest issue – newsroom morale. Meeting staff formally and informally, answering their questions about the paper's future direction, the disparity in punishment for the three journalists concerned, working to keep the vibrancy of the paper and newsroom going, how we should respond to questions about the episode ... I devoted my time to get cracking on these issues.

I began to realise that these measures could only go part way to restore the newsroom to its glory days. A piece in the jigsaw was missing. That piece had to come from the editors and it had to be demonstrated to the newsroom. We had to show by example what we would do if another dicey situation involving a high-profile personality was to present itself again. We did not have to wait long before a story with very similar traits landed on our laps.

A tip-off from a high-level source told us that a grandson of property magnate Ng Teng Fong had been found with a gunshot wound in his head in a hotel in Peshawar, Pakistan. We had the name, and information on when and where the tragedy had happened. All were confirmed by the Pakistani police and the hotel, but the missing link was whether he was indeed Ng Teng Fong's grandson. Positive ID of the young man's relationship to the Ng family was the crucial piece of information needed to make the decision whether the story should be on Page One. It was an eerie throwback to the Toh Chin Chye story. With a newsroom watching on intently to see how we would play this story, we went back to the source and asked this question: "We can't confirm that he is Ng's grandson. You have a source we can check with?" The source said that Ambassador Tommy Koh should know. Citing confidentiality, Ambassador Koh declined to confirm the identity of the 22-year-old man, but he did say he was helping to get a man flown home, without confirming that this was the grandson.

A helpful clue, but it was not the clincher. The editors decided it was worth taking the risk and publishing the story.

We reasoned that Ambassador Koh did not deny the story and his help had to have been sought because the person involved was linked to one of Singapore's most prominent families. There was, however, still that 0.0001 per cent chance that the injured man could be someone else. The green light for Page One with the headline "Tycoon Ng Teng Fong's Grandson Found Shot" was given. The paper went to press. The newsroom was tense, waiting nervously to see if there would be a reaction.

I drove to Jurong Country Club, sat down at the restaurant facing the expansive golf course and waited. Nothing happened. I knew the story was accurate and the heavy cloud of excessive caution that had enveloped the newsroom after the Toh Chin Chye fiasco had been lifted. What nobody knew was that I had written my letter of resignation, with instructions to my secretary, Doreen Sabai, to hand it to the editor-in-chief if there was a backlash. I went back to the office, shredded the letter and heaved a sigh of relief.

With that walk on the tightrope, we buried the spectre of the Toh Chin Chye affair. However, the pain still persists. Yan Chong declined my request to interview him for this chapter. "I don't want to go there," he said rather abruptly. Ken Jalleh was very helpful in providing details to flesh out the crisis. Ivan was uncontactable. All three have, however, gone on to do well in their careers. Yan Chong moved on to become energy correspondent at Reuters and, later, director of Thomson Reuters Oil Research & Forecast in Asia. Ken reinvented himself in a marketing role in Singapore Press Holdings, and Ivan became the editor of TNP and then associate editor of *The Straits Times*.

CHAPTER 6

Indian Fever
And TNP's role in it

Abhijit Nag was gauche. Earnest and soft-spoken, he was not suave or street smart as some might expect a journalist to be, but he could use words to dramatic effect.

We were looking for journalists to launch *The New Paper* when we asked him and a few others to go to New Delhi for an interview in December 1987. We got them to take written tests. Abhijit produced a piece that touched a nerve. Headlined "Toilet Baby", it was about a newborn found in a toilet. Although it seemed a Gothic flight of fantasy, it was grounded in reality. Such was life in his hometown.

He was from Calcutta and he was no fan of the city. Years later, he would tell me exactly why, without skipping a beat:

> A congested metropolis, the former capital of the British Raj had fallen on hard times and was taking it hard, abounding in poets, agitators and beggars. It was a city where cultural soirees at night alternated with angry demonstrations and running battles between the police and stone-throwing agitators during the day. Where young men remained unemployed for years because businesses and industries were shutting down and moving out following strikes and agitations

by the communists who had been voted to power in the state of West Bengal of which Calcutta was the capital. It was a city of pavement dwellers, where destitutes slept on the streets, and abandoned babies didn't even make the news.

The interview panel was impressed with Abhijit's turn of phrase, the elegance of his language and his uncanny ability to write short, bold and accurate headlines that would be perfect for a paper like *The New Paper*. It was conceptualised as a paper that was big on colourful pictures and graphics, and less fixated on essays. For a Singapore whose very notion of a newspaper had been shackled to *The Straits Times*, *The New Paper* was intended to pioneer a new form of journalism that captured the spirit of the times, to examine and understand an era that Singapore was entering with some trepidation. A younger population with lots of money to spend was hungry for fresh avenues to let off steam, albeit with some kind of discretion and control. And perhaps, they wanted a new kind of newspaper. On 26 July 1988, this new blend of experiment and experience bore fruit, with an influx of talent from India and some other countries helping us Singaporeans to embark on this new journey.

Most of the journalists we interviewed during those foggy and frosty days in New Delhi showed skills and traits that were in short supply in Singapore, especially the hunger to excel. Prominent among those we engaged were Ravindra Kumar, who returned to India after his three-year stint in Singapore and is now editor and managing director of *The Statesman*; Tamal Mukherjee, who went on to become a senior producer with Singapore's Channel NewsAsia; Soutik Biswas, who is now India correspondent for the BBC; and Ravi Shankar Narasimhan, who led a nomadic life until he joined *China Daily*, where he is in charge of its overseas editions.

In the corridors of gossip in Singapore Press Holdings (SPH), which publishes *The New Paper* and other titles in English, Chinese, Malay and Tamil, mischievous whispers seemed to be gaining ground. "Balji is running an Indian mafia," some would complain during lunch breaks and drinking sprees.

The reality was something quite different. It was SR Nathan, SPH's executive chairman at the time, who suggested we look to India for the journalists we needed. He even had his contact in Delhi place advertisements in newspapers and arranged the interviews for us. The pay-and-perks package was attractive, with monthly salaries of around S$3,000, bonuses, a trip back home and rent paid for by the company. The Indian expat journalists more than returned the favour with their commitment, work attitude and, above all else, the quality of their work. They were all recruited as sub-editors but they also wrote commentaries and went on reporting assignments. They impressed the American and Australian editors, few of whom had encountered journalists from India before. Among the western expats who had been specially recruited to simplify the language of reporters' copy was John Lang, who had been a former senior editor with the magazine *US News & World Report*. With disarming candour, John said: "You should sack all of us and recruit more Indian journalists. Their salaries are not high, their language is good, and they are willing workers."

Soutik Biswas supplied some useful socio-economic and political context to the "exodus" of Indian journalists at the time. India, he said, was a very different country at the time when *The New Paper* was looking to recruit journalists, and the paper was able to attract Indian journalists to leave their jobs to work in Singapore. "It was a desperate time, and desperate times lead to desperate measures, like leaving the country and looking for greener pastures."

He goes on to explain just how desperate things were in India then:

> The 1980s and 1990s were our worst decades. The economy was in the dumps. The Indian Army stormed the Golden Temple to flush out Sikh separatists, (and this was) followed by the revenge killing of Prime Minister Indira Gandhi by her Sikh bodyguards. The anti-Sikh riots convulsed Delhi. And thousands of people in the city of Bhopal were killed after toxic gases leaked from a chemical factory, the world's worst industrial accident. Calcutta was in shambles after more than a decade of uninterrupted Communist rule, with industrial strikes and electricity blackouts.

Calcutta native Abhijit, like many of the Indians who arrived in 1988, thrived in a Singapore where street traffic was never held up by protest marches, where strikes were inconceivable, where jobs were so plentiful that locals couldn't fill them all and foreigners had to be brought in. *The New Paper* newsroom, when it was launched in 1988, was highly cosmopolitan, employing Americans, Britons, Australians, Indians, Filipinos and Malaysians, as well as Singaporeans.

Their hardworking nature, skills and ability to turn around an article without fuss amazed many editors at *The New Paper*. Patrick Daniel, then editor of the *Business Times*, was quick to spot the potential of the Indians and sparked the second Indian wave by recruiting many commentary writers, reporters and sub-editors. Soon after, *The Straits Times* followed suit. Indian fever was well and truly stoked. As Soutik Biswas noted of that period:

> The irony is that it wasn't really a bad time to be a journalist in India. But many of the people ... were stellar desk hands with good experience as sub-editors and section editors. Singapore offered better pay and a higher quality of life, and many moved to escape the grim realities at home, like many other Indians who emigrated to the West around that time.

It was actually then Prime Minister Goh Chok Tong who had said in 1993 that he wanted to create an Indian fever. That was five years before *The New Paper*'s own Indian wave. On a national scale, the India-Singapore bromance is now in full bloom, with Singapore's cheerleading efforts seeing India roll out the red carpet for all ten ASEAN states to attend the South Asian giant's Republic Day in New Delhi, and meetings with Prime Minister Narendra Modi and other top officials in 2018.

The India-Singapore connection has come a long way with economic, diplomatic, security, strategic and social ties being expanded at a fast clip. Economic and trade links are the headline-making news, but the sub-text and the more geo-political story is about security and strategic relationship with India seen as a counter weight to a China that is showing off its muscle, especially in the South China Sea where some ASEAN nations and China have competing claims.

The wooing of India has opened Singapore's stubborn immigration gates to a new class of emigres and expats from the subcontinent: bankers, businessmen, professionals and IT gurus. Their presence has become visible with modern-day luxe ghettos being formed in small parts of the Singapore landscape. If you go to the Meyer Road area in the east, their presence is unmistakable, with the smell of curries and the sound of Bollywood songs attacking your senses. They are the third Indian wave. The first happened when the British colonialists brought convict labour to Singapore to build roads, buildings and other infrastructure; the second came when independent Singapore wanted to fill a chronic need for construction workers and cleaners; and the final surge is happening now with high-end Indians coming in droves to fuel our economy. An Indian expatriate who took up Singapore citizenship describes them as the "Orchard Road Indians", referring to their high spending power. This has, in turn, smashed the stereotype of the foreign Indian, Amrit Barman says in his book, *India Fever: The New Indian Professional in Singapore*.[1] These Indians receive VIP treatment in upper-crust boutiques, top-class restaurants and pubs. My wife, Uma, experienced this at first hand. Mistaking her for an Indian national, the salesgirl at Tangs in Orchard Road was extremely hospitable and courteous. "Are you an expatriate?" the lady asked her. Uma had to disappoint her by saying no and leaving the department store without buying anything.

SPH was quick to spot the spending power of this group of expatriates and launched a free weekly newspaper in October 2008 targeted at this free-spending group and the advertisers who wanted to reach them. The working title for the weekly was catchy and direct: *IndEx* – "Ind" for Indian and "Ex" for

---

[1] Amrit Barman, *India Fever: The New Indian Professional in Singapore* (Singapore Indian Association, 2009).

expatriates. Wiser minds, including that of the late Senior Minister of State for Foreign Affairs, Balaji Sadasivan, counselled against this title as it might cause uneasiness in the Singaporean Indian community. Finally, SPH settled on the title *tabla!* Run on a shoe-string budget, the publication has continued to survive despite a slowing economy and declining print revenue.

Several of the Indian journalists who joined *The Straits Times* and *Business Times* have stayed on with SPH, adding value to the papers' editorial coverage. *The Straits Times*' economics specialist, Vikram Khanna, and *The Straits Times*' regional commentator, Ravi Velloor, are heavy hitters with their insightful analyses which add depth and breadth to the newspapers they write for. Their "brand-name" commentaries continue to be valued by the elite.

The journalist I wrote about at the beginning of this chapter, Abhijit Nag, decided to stay on in Singapore, even though he left *The New Paper* soon after 2000. He now works for a magazine called *India Se*. I have a soft spot for Abhijit. His introverted nature and his writing flair drew me to him. In many ways, Singapore had spoilt him. He keeps moaning about the decadent state of his birthplace, Calcutta, and lights up each time the conversation turns to Singapore, especially the National Library, where he drowns himself in new books and old classics. Singapore, where he has a Housing and Development Board (HDB) flat and a coveted permanent residency, is his home for now. Abhijit finds solace in a line from a Walter Savage Landor poem: "I strove with none, for none was worthy of my strife."

Exactly 30 years after he first arrived here chasing the rainbow of life, Abhijit now sees a new Singapore, a Singapore that is changing dramatically. It is getting more expensive, the city is getting overcrowded and at 62, he knows that getting a well-paying job in a news organisation like SPH is a pipe dream. He recalls a Rolling Stones song: "You can't always get what you want." The only craft he knows, journalism, looks so different now as well. Clickbait and search engine optimisation are more in demand now than a well-turned phrase. The thrill, he says, is gone.

CHAPTER 7

Big, Bold and Sometimes Ugly
An apology is in store

BIG, bold, sexy, sensational, intriguing, teasing, bruising, striking, over the top, naughty, serious, to the point, novel, inventive, *avant garde*, eye catching, lip smacking, crisp, scathing, attention grabbing, hurtful, head turner, path breaker, blinding, salacious …

I could go on and on describing that one obvious obsession of *The New Paper*: the Page One headline. The paper lived or died on the impact of those scant and terse words. Get the headline right and the paper's sales would skyrocket. Get it wrong and sales would bomb. You loved it or you hated it.

The best accolade came from the unlikeliest quarter, the British media, better known for criticising the Singapore media as pro-government. Peter Preston, a former editor of *The Guardian* newspaper, writing in *The Observer* in 1998, said of *The New Paper*: "Its front page is always a single hit. Usually a picture and a superimposed headline, but occasionally just type: Plots. Lies. Twisted Words."

When the criticism came from within, the words hit home a lot harder and their sting was all the more acid. The unexpected source was TNP reporter, Angeline Song. Her criticism hit hardest of all because of her devotion to the newspaper. She was a pocket whirlwind, an indefatigable reporter whose latent but no less impassioned *chilli padi* core would burst out for all to see when she was chasing exclusive stories on disadvantaged Singaporeans, people who had slid involuntarily into a bottomless pit of poverty, crime, drugs and sex abuse. A group often ignored, sidelined and even deliberately shunned by a seemingly thrusting population marching with single-minded focus to make the country a beacon of economic success. Angeline told me by email: "As a TNP reporter, I always tried to conduct my interviews with great care, responsibility and empathy. And it would be with heightened sensitivity for a story involving an illness that is often misunderstood."

HIV was the subject of one of her front page stories. It became memorable for all the wrong reasons. She had managed to get permission to visit the ward in the Communicable Disease Centre where HIV patients stayed, and to interview the caregivers. She was possibly the first reporter to be allowed in. Given the fear and stigma attached to the disease, gaining access had taken much trust-building. The caregivers and those who managed the ward had done such a wonderful job, she recalled. "Not only did I discover a rare place that provided its patients with physical relief but it was also a place which – extraordinarily, given the circumstances – exuded cheer and hope."

She took the utmost care to reflect those qualities. "I tried to write it as sensitively and responsibly as possible," she said. The photographer assigned took many shots of a smiling caregiver in the ward. The resulting package covered five inside pages and was as she had planned, but the front page headline all but shouted "Death Ward" over a photo of an unsmiling caregiver, which readers might have interpreted as downcast, sober or even grim.[1] The killer was that "Death Ward" headline.

Distressed, incensed and on the verge of tears, Angeline told the Big Desk: "How could you *do* this! This is a place of hope and you have turned it into a place of death! All for a headline like this! Nobody will ever speak to us again!" She recalled in her email:

> I remember crying at my desk and seriously considering leaving TNP or even journalism altogether. I felt that my professional and personal integrity had been compromised. For me, as a journalist, building contacts and maintaining the trust of newsmakers was vital. And as a human being, I felt immensely saddened to have been involved indirectly in hurting courageous, inspiring folk.

Fortunately, she did not leave TNP. At least, not then. She continued reporting, eventually joining the Big Desk and spending a total of 15 years on the job. "As a pioneer TNPer, the paper's culture was and, in many ways, still is in my DNA … Still, I took the lessons I had learnt at TNP, and its ethos, with me when I started my own PR and advertising agency in Auckland, New Zealand." She left for "a more balanced lifestyle in another country or culture that was not so single-mindedly focused on simply achieving economic progress." A few years later, TNP sought her out and she rejoined the Big Desk. Later on, she rejoined for a third stint, as correspondent. In her email of June 2018, she added: "Today, I am a postdoctoral researcher,

---

[1] "Death Ward", *The New Paper*, 7 December 1991.

conference and retreat speaker and published author. In some way or other, all these have been influenced and informed by my time at TNP."

Her story illustrates not only her distress but the dedication that she and many others in this newsroom had for their craft, and consequentially, the sometime intensely personal attacks they had to deal with when their work drew flak from the public or strong reactions from official sources. That Page One, which was our prime circulation driver, could at one and the same time be a lightning conductor for the harshest criticism.

The reason for our obsession with the Page One headline is obvious: to seize your attention in a world crying out to be noticed, to capture a slice of what little time you have, to show and tell. And yes, to sell. TNP's lifeblood depended on getting people out of their workplaces and homes to buy our newspaper from vendors in the streets. TNP was not like Singapore's main newspapers, which were mostly delivered to regular paying subscribers at home or wherever they worked. The 70 cents that a reader paid for our newspaper did not factor in the cost to them in time and convenience. They had to make a conscious decision to buy the paper.

Finding a niche in a marketplace weaned on the powerful, all-encompassing banyan tree called *The Straits Times* became a matter of survival. What is Page One? What is the headline? These watchwords were propagated in the newsroom with a messianic zeal that had to be experienced to be believed. TNP was an afternoon newspaper that was meant to hit the streets by 11am. Not only did this limit its shelf life, it also limited the timespan of its coverage of the events of the day and also the opportunity to sell the paper. Rainy days could spell disaster as most people would be inclined to stay indoors. Holidays could be even worse as potential readers would be away from Singapore.

The journalist at the sharp end of this incessant preaching was Ken Jalleh, the man given the unenviable responsibility of being on top of the news of the day – from local to foreign to sports to showbiz. We didn't believe in segregating these interests under the usual labels. All these sections came under our Big Desk, with Ken as the Big Man to run it. The thinking behind this loose merger of all desks was simple. TNP's Page One didn't discriminate. Wherever the biggest news came from, whether it was from our own journalists covering local, foreign, sports events, or from news agencies, it could make it to Page One. What *The Straits Times* picked as its Page One lead would almost invariably be the most important story of the day; TNP would gun for the most interesting. That freed its editors to run with nearly any type of story. It could be a political story about the abrupt but calm and measured way in which President Ong Teng Cheong announced his decision in May 1999 not to stand for re-election. His biggest gripe: that civil servants had put up obstacles when he sought a detailed breakdown of the nation's physical assets such as buildings and other forms of sovereign wealth, and that some civil servants had found him a nuisance. TNP reported that historical press conference in the form of a Page One editorial with the headline "Thank you, Mr President … for discussing openly the problems you had faced".[2]

A Page One headline that could have landed the paper in trouble with the political leadership was published the day after Mr SR Nathan, a former SPH executive chairman, became

---

[2] "Thank you, Mr President … for discussing openly the problems you had faced", *The New Paper*, 17 July 1999.

President Nathan in 1999. We found an old picture of Mr Nathan, in sarong and singlet, standing outside his house. Our headline read: "Sarong President".[3] Soon after the paper hit the streets, I got a call from a Ministry of Communications and Information official telling me that several members of the public had called the ministry expressing outrage at what they considered an insensitive headline and inappropriate picture. So much for a public who always complained that the media was under government control. The editors had gone ahead with the headline and picture because they felt these showed the real character of this very down-to-earth man. Mr Nathan served two terms, 12 years in all, as Singapore's Head of State and he is still remembered that way. The editors sought to test his reaction and sent a news editor to talk to him about that Page One. As they had expected, he was not the least bothered and a potentially sticky situation dissolved into nothing. Mr Nathan, the country's longest-serving president, left office in 2011 and died in 2016 at the age of 92.

My all-time favourite TNP Page One featured a two-word headline for a medical story that was published in 1997: "Mrs Virgin".[4] The report featured interviews with two married women who had failed to conceive after five years of marriage and had absolutely no clue that they and their husbands had been having sex the wrong way. The women's gynaecologists had examined them and found no medical reason for their inability to conceive. The women then consulted a sex doctor who dropped this bombshell: they were still virgins. Until then, they had no clue that they were doing it the wrong way. The headline was, shall we say, conceived by an artist, Simon Ang. In conventional

---

[3] "Sarong President", *The New Paper*, 19 August 1999.
[4] "Mrs Virgin", *The New Paper*, 8 November 1997.

newspapers, headlines are written by sub-editors, but TNP wanted everyone – from reporters to photographers to artists to editors – to come up with pithy and catchy headlines that would convey the most crucial aspect of a story. Such headlines often stopped people on the streets in their daily rush and made them pause to buy the paper and read the story.

That day, when I walked into the newsroom at 6am, it happened to be Simon's turn to pick what he thought should be the Page One lead, choose the visual and write the headline. Simon said he was just "scribbling some roughs". It was spontaneous. "I just came up with 'Mrs Virgin' but I wasn't sure how this would fit into the whole story," he added. He was rather sheepish about his headline, unsure if it would be accepted. He tried to hide it but I asked him what he had doodled on that piece of paper he was keeping covered. He showed it to me, reluctantly.

Wow! What a zinger! With just two words, Simon had captured the essence of the story. It was intriguing and teasing, and most importantly, it was accurate. I asked him why he had hesitated to show it to me. He said: "I am just an artist … like a second-class citizen in a newsroom. I was afraid that the headline might be rejected." How wrong he was! Not only did it make Page One, but it was chosen by SPH editors as Headline of the Year – the first time a journalist other than a reporter, sub-editor or editor had claimed that honour.

There is a Page One headline that I will regret for the rest of my life. It appeared on 31 March 1994. "Go To Hell" it screamed, over a photograph of a downcast national soccer coach, Ken Worden. He had quit abruptly and inexplicably with just five days to go before a crucial Malaysia Cup match against the Malaysian state of Kelantan.

In an editorial accompanying the headline, the paper said: "You have let us down. And in the worst way possible – with just five days to go before a crucial match against Kelantan. You, the man who always had the last word, were nowhere to be found. Don't take the coward's way out. Come clean before you flee."

The furious blowback from several staff as well as angry members of the public was immediate and pulled no punches. One reporter invoked religion to attack the headline. Her argument: "Hell is where the devil lives and Worden is no devil. We really don't know why he quit so suddenly. Even if he was really a bad guy, nobody should wish that kind of an eventuality on another human being," she said in an email to me. Even Prime Minister Goh Chok Tong sent word that such extreme admonishment of foreigners was not good for Singapore's efforts to persuade them to work and live here. Ken Worden was from Britain. He had quit three months into a two-year contract as head coach. He continued to coach teams in Malaysia, Myanmar and Australia, but has since retired from football.

Looking back at my career, especially in my autumn years, this headline comes back to haunt me. We were too preoccupied with wanting to reflect the furore among the football fans, but there are no two ways about that headline. It was wrong. Ken Worden, wherever you are, I apologise for having rubbished you like that.

Soccer was the subject of another Page One headline, but this time with praise all round for its daring creativity. Just two words: "Tonight How?" Those two words on an otherwise blank Page One didn't scream. They were in fairly small black type and, as an afterthought, a picture of a football with the words "see page 2" were added at the right-hand corner. The germ of the idea originated in splash designer R Jegathesan's head. He had planned to use it as a small teaser in one of the sports pages. An editor who always wanted something special, something different, spotted it and wanted to reserve it for Page One.

It was a Saturday in 1993. Malaysia Cup fever had taken over the island, with only one topic on the lips of soccer fans: Will Singapore win? How many goals? Who will score? TNP wanted to dive into this mood and have a cover page reflecting that fever.

That "Tonight How?" cover was the result,[5] but one niggling thought troubled the editors. Would football fans bite? Would they buy the paper? Big Desk editor, Ken Jalleh, went out for a smoke and came back with a stroke of genius: "Let's get the fans to play editor and use the generous white space on Page One to write their own headlines." It worked. The paper sold out that Saturday, and that night, many fans were seen at the National Stadium waving the page to show off their headlines.

The last word in this chapter belongs to Ken, a pioneer of the paper whose love affair with it is still as passionate as it was three decades ago:

> In defending, evangelising or justifying TNP to its many detractors, I've often likened the paper's approach to a shopping mall. Look at Page One as the mall's window dressing, screaming huge discounts. Step inside, however, and you'll discover cafes for interaction, libraries or bookshops for enlightenment, cinemas for entertainment. Discerning readers would sense, over time, that there was more to TNP than its face. Stepping inside, readers found a conscious effort to simplify complex government policies, done with brevity and clarity.

---

[5] "Tonight How?", *The New Paper*, 9 October 1995.

CHAPTER 8

TODAY Bets on Goh Chok Tong
Chairman Cheng makes split-second decision

T he telephone call could not have come at a more opportune moment. The woman at the other end of the line said that her boss, the chief of a headhunting firm, would like to meet me in his office. I had just marked ten years as editor of *The New Paper* and was becoming increasingly restless. I had been considering and talking about a change of job. Thinking aloud in a column in TNP on 7 August 1999, I wondered what I should do next: with 50 years of my life gone (30 of them being a workaholic, with a daughter planning to get married the next year, heart bypass surgery behind me and energy levels dropping by the day), I had been asking myself whether it was time to step off the Singapore Treadmill and pamper myself a little.

These thoughts hid the real sentiment I was experiencing at that time. My job in the newsroom was highly satisfying and rewarding, but it had become too familiar a grind. Most days, I was doing the same thing over and over again. Getting up at 4am, reading the newspapers, communicating by phone with the staff who were already in the office, rushing to Times House by 6am, scanning the important and sensitive stories, talking to production and circulation people ... the routine was getting to me.

I needed a break, a change. I asked the editor-in-chief, Cheong Yip Seng, to consider posting me to India as *The Straits Times*' correspondent, or transferring me to Singapore Press Holdings' circulation department, an area that I felt would offer me a fresh creative lease on my life. As expected, Cheong said "no".

So that phone call from the headhunting company, Amrop, was a godsend. At the interview with the boss of the company, Tan Soo Jin, I found out that they were looking for someone to head a new Singapore newspaper. No other details were given.

Things then moved at breakneck speed. The CEO of Mediacorp, Lee Hup Seng, called me for an interview. Mediacorp chairman, Cheng Wai Keung, arranged for us to have a breakfast chat – just the two of us – on a Sunday in 2000 at his home. I must have spent an hour with Wai Keung and came away impressed with his understanding of how the reader's mind works. As I left his bungalow, one of his statements stuck in my mind. "Balji, the paper has to get into the homes. Going to the MRT stations and offices must just be a cover [for our actual plans]. The real battle to convince advertisers to put their money in this paper must be fought in the homes. *The Straits Times* has entrenched themselves there. Take the battle to them."

These were not just fighting words, but smart ones. Wai Keung, who was also the boss of retail and property giant Wing Tai Holdings, knew what it meant to fight. He learnt it all on the mean streets of Hong Kong, where survival depended on taking the fight to one's rivals.

At that initial meeting with him, our distribution strategy for *TODAY* was born. With chief operating officer Philip Koh at the helm of production and distribution, a covert plan was drawn up to get the paper into people's homes, while the world was told that TODAY would be made available mainly at MRT stations and offices.

It had to do with how the mind works. Each morning, when the bleary-eyed reader opened his door and saw *The Straits Times* and *TODAY* on his doorstep, the sight of those two newspapers together would send out a powerful signal that *TODAY* was on par with *The Straits Times*. That strategy may have seemed more symbolic, but it worked. It made readers and advertisers take us seriously. They got the message that *TODAY* meant business, and that it was here to stay.

The team collected names and addresses of the "who's who" in politics, advertising, business, academia and government, and began delivering the paper to their homes from Monday to Saturday. It was a massive operation: vendors who could be trusted to deliver the paper to the right addresses at the right time had to be found, and they had to be trained to deal with security officers in condominiums who might not let them in. In such instances, Philip and company had to go and meet the condominium management committees and assure them our people were performing a legitimate service. In some instances, we had to talk to acquaintances who lived in the targeted condominiums and try to convince them to put some pressure on their management committees to allow our vendors in. We launched on 10 November 2000, and within two years, we had managed to get into nearly all the homes we had targeted.

Soon after that initial meeting in his home, Wai Keung came back to play another defining role in *TODAY*'s progress and eventual survival. The editorial and advertising teams had met to decide on the newspaper's editorial approach. It was an unconventional way of approaching an editorial philosophy, having the key people sit around a table where copies of *The Straits Times*, *Business Times*, *The New Paper* and a new entrant, *Streats*, were lined up, with a space left for TODAY. The freesheet, *Streats*, was published in September 2000 by Singapore Press Holdings (SPH) just two months before TODAY hit the streets. Its last edition was released on 31 December 2004.

Our team had decided against commissioning readership and marketing surveys. For one thing, we were not prepared to spend on surveys; for another, we suspected that people often avoided telling the truth when asked for their views. We were also convinced that such research was usually conducted in too perfunctory a fashion. Some of us were already familiar with the prevailing methodology of readership surveys. Showing interviewees the masthead of a paper, a researcher would ask: "Did you read this yesterday?" If the answer was "yes", they were considered "readers". Follow-up questions to establish whether those interviewees were really readers were never asked. Such methods continue to this day and still manage to persuade newspapers and advertising agencies to shell out huge sums for what is essentially a flimsy construct of superficial results.

After we had agreed on the positioning of the various newspapers, each one of us present had to answer two questions: Was there space for a new paper like TODAY? If there was no space, could we create one? We did not get to the second question, as some of us agreed that the missing space was for a paper that was prepared to be bold and to inject analysis into its news reports, not just to deliver only the "who", "what", "when" and "how", but also the "why" of the news.

One of the individuals present asked a very pertinent question: Will the Singapore government be amenable to this type of journalism, as it had spoken out publicly on many occasions against mixing news with analysis and comment; the separation of news and analysis and comment had to be like that between church and state. But I was confident that Prime Minister Goh Chok Tong, who had come to power ten years earlier in 1990 with a publicly-stated mission to move away from Lee Kuan Yew's top-down approach, would not interfere. We bet on him and won. Not once in my first three years at TODAY was there a call from the Prime Minister's Office to complain about our style of reporting.

I am, however, getting ahead of the story of how TODAY was born. Ernest Wong took over from Lee Hup Seng as Mediacorp CEO shortly after I joined the team. When chairman Wai Keung, Ernest, the paper's COO, Philip Koh, and I met to discuss our paper's editorial concept one Saturday afternoon, we did not begin on the same page. Ernest was deeply impressed with what he had just seen on a visit to the Modern Times Group in Sweden. This was the group that had launched the free newspaper revolution with *Metro*. He was keen to follow their model – a stripped-down version of a conventional newspaper. Modern Times kept *Metro*'s manpower strength to a bare minimum and restricted the number of pages to a low of 28.

Ernest saw TODAY as a downmarket freesheet with short stories and big pictures; in other words, a newspaper that commuters would skim and chuck into the bin after their train ride. At that Saturday meeting, he said that TODAY should not go upmarket, and should keep the number of pages to a minimum and its circulation small. This went directly against what the editorial and advertising teams had decided on. I made it plain that the paper had to be credible to readers and attractive to advertisers, especially the big boys in the business. With advertisements being TODAY's only source of revenue, our survival would be threatened if we could not attract the likes of DBS Bank, Singapore Airlines and Great Eastern. The discussion became heated. I reminded the group that I had come from ten years of editing The New Paper, a newspaper that many regarded as a throwaway, and one that many top advertisers had refused to even consider as an option. I remember telling them: "I can do such a paper with my eyes closed and hands tied behind my back. All I need is a letter from Ernest saying we should take that route."

That was when our worldly-wise chairman stepped in, took Ernest out of the meeting room and came back alone with these cryptic but decisive words: "Balji, you go your way." Those few words made the difference as TODAY managed to bring in top advertisers, including Great Eastern, Hewlett Packard, Dell, Carrefour, Canon, Revlon, L'Oreal and HSBC.

Ernest proved to be a gentleman. My fear that the boss-employee relationship would sour was unfounded. During my first run at the helm of TODAY, not once did he show any hostility, implicit or otherwise, towards me. In fact, when I told him that I would leave after the end of my three-year contract, he was surprised and tried to persuade me to stay on for two more years.

After TODAY cleared the hurdle of deciding on the paper's editorial positioning, more daunting issues began to appear.

The day before the *TODAY* board was due to meet the media to announce details of the launch, ComfortDelgro, one of the paper's four investors, pulled out. At about that time, a good Samaritan called to warn me about the problems I would face with the printer. "If I were you," he said, "I would visit the printer and ask some important questions."

I had only one question for the printer, Kim Hup Lee (KHL): Can you guarantee that the paper will appear on time? The management at the printing plant all looked down, not wanting to give me a direct answer. It was just two weeks to our launch date and the *TODAY* management went into overdrive to identify the kinks and to look into resolving them.

Our team had been so preoccupied with recruitment, meeting potential advertisers and launching the computer systems for both the editorial and advertising teams that we had collectively taken our eyes off the ball and failed to recognise the printing storm that was brewing. KHL was started in 1978 and had built a reputation for itself as a good commercial printer for magazines and brochures. But it had zero experience in printing newspapers, never mind churning out 300,000 copies every day six days a week and getting it done with a narrow window no wider than four or five hours. They had bought new machines from Germany to give us the capability of offering colour on every page, something that even publishing giant SPH, the parent company of *The Straits Times*, could not deliver.

There was one huge problem. KHL did not have enough trained staff to operate the state-of-the-art machines. Angela Chia, the liaison manager for printing, said: "The staff were trained to print magazines. They were not familiar with handling newspaper printing, and were also not familiar with such newspaper density at such speed."

The reckoning came in the early hours of the paper's launch on 10 November 2000. The entire production team, journalists, photographers, sales and marketing managers, hurried into taxis and cars outside our office at Clifford Centre in Raffles Place, and headed to KHL's printing factory in far-flung Loyang.

We were not the only ones there. Several trucks and cars, some of them naively showing SPH car labels, were parked outside the printing site. A bunch of men still wearing their name tags were lounging around drinking coffee. We knew the war had started. They wanted to know our distribution strategy and the best way was to follow our trucks as they left Loyang. They would trail our lorries every morning. Their moves were recorded for posterity by a reporter from Channel NewsAsia, who walked up, aimed her microphone at them as the camera zoomed in on their name tags and asked what they were doing there. "We are having coffee," they all said.

At the printing site, the normally taciturn Philip Koh was pacing the floor, gesticulating, talking and sometimes shouting. I realised there was nothing we could do to speed things up. I went home and waited and waited for a message to say that the machines had started rolling. *Zilch.* By the time I got up, there was a message to say printing had started, then another to say that the presses had stopped because of some kinks in the system.

SPH's kill-the-rival machinery went into high gear. Calls were made to advertising agencies and advertisers telling them how unreliable *TODAY* was, and asking: "Do you still want to advertise with them?" Our phones rang incessantly with panic-stricken and angry advertisers threatening to cancel their orders. We had to appease them with explanations and even offers of steep discounts for their advertisements. We made sure that all our staff had all the answers to questions that were likely to be raised by friends, newsmakers and others. The Mediacorp Press board had to be mollified, and being linked to Temasek Holdings, the Temasek management and government people had to be briefed.

The printing presses continued to have hiccups, but these became fewer and fewer. Meanwhile, other storms began to gather on the horizon ...

CHAPTER 9

TODAY Arrives, SPH Miscalculates
And media history is made

The senior team at *TODAY* was tired, upset and angry. What was to have been a pivotal moment in their professional lives as they geared up for the big battle with the bastion of print journalism, *The Straits Times*, was crumbling in front of them. The inaugural edition of the upstart just refused to get off the printing presses on the morning of 10 November 2000. Never before had the printer, KHL, had to print 300,000 copies of a newspaper a day six days a week, much less get it done within four to five hours. Its expertise was in printing magazines to more forgiving deadlines. The higher the sun rose in the sky, the more downcast the staff became. *TODAY's* chief operating officer, Philip Koh, was probably the only one who showed little emotion as he worked tirelessly through the early hours of the morning with KHL's owner, Lim Geok Khoon, to get the paper out and onto the streets. Philip's training as a naval officer helped immensely.

The presses would start, print a few thousand copies, then stop. This start-go-stop-restart nightmare went on late into the afternoon with the staff increasingly mortified over what should have been a significant moment in Singapore's media history. Both print and TV monopolies had been ended, the result of the government's declared grand plan to liberalise Singapore media. "Proliferate" might have been a more apt word than "liberalise". Singapore Press Holdings had been granted a licence to start two TV channels, previously the jealously guarded turf of government-owned Mediacorp. SPH Mediaworks was launched in 2000, but after running up huge losses had to give up one of its two channels, Channel U, which was absorbed by Mediacorp. Now, Mediacorp was bidding to break into SPH's monopoly on print. From the word go, both went for each other's throats, fighting tooth and nail to grab a larger share of the advertising pie and a bigger slice of the readership cake.

TODAY's initial printing fiasco was manna from heaven for SPH. Like a well-oiled war machine on overdrive, SPH zoomed into the offices of advertisers and advertising agencies rubbishing the newcomer's ability to be a viable and dependable product.

TODAY fought back on two fronts. On the PR front, we reached out to the ad people, explaining what had happened with the inaugural edition of the paper and why we faced these technical problems. Even the boss of KHL, Lim Geok Khoon, was roped in to meet the ad people. This way, he could explain the intricacies of the printing processes and the issues his company was dealing with. COO Philip Koh and his ad sales team fanned out to mollify advertising agencies. As CEO of Mediacorp Press, I met our major advertisers with just one appeal: if you don't give us a chance, you will return to the dark ages of doing business with an uncompromising and stifling monopoly.

The printing issues persisted for a few months. All this while, the team proactively informed our clients of the problems and measures they were taking to resolve them. They sensed that our clients were willing to give us the benefit of the doubt. All this made us realise that *TODAY* needed its own person on site whose sole responsibility was to work with the printer and keep the team informed. Sultan Ahmed, who had worked with the short-lived newspaper, the *Singapore Monitor*, in the 1980s, was well-versed in printing matters and the needs of the editorial departments. He was our man on the ground, telling the key people at *TODAY* what to look out for and what needed to be done to keep the presses humming. Sultan was also an early warning system, sounding the alert on possible problems ahead, very valuable indeed as the team could plan its operations accordingly.

SPH wanted to know our distribution strategy, and the best way was to follow our lorries as they left KHL every morning. In the early hours of 10 November 2000, as *TODAY* struggled to get the first issue out, SPH's distribution teams were already at our printing site in Loyang. A few trucks bearing the SPH logo were stationed outside, keeping a watching brief.

This failed to bother most of our team, but behind our mild amusement was the serious realisation that the cat-and-mouse games had begun. Some in the team were SPH alumni with first-hand experience of the print giant as a bulldozer, fully capable of knocking the competition out of shape. They knew it was war. Whose blood, I wondered, would be on the floor? *TODAY* would be distributed at subway stations, especially in the Central Business District, and delivered to selected offices and homes. The content would be what *The Straits Times* (ST) would not, and could not, deliver. The insurgent would not be brazenly pro-government: it would mix analysis with news. The editors discussed the content of the inaugural edition at some length. Would we get into trouble with the government? That was one of the questions posed. Possible, I said, but I was betting on Prime Minister Goh Chok Tong to give us the space we needed.

My instincts were proven right. In my three years as the paper's editor-in-chief and CEO of Mediacorp Press, not once did I get a call from the Prime Minister's Office complaining about anything we had published. ST, however, did not let it rest. I got wind of information that some ST editors had told David Lim, then Acting Minister of Information, Communications and the Arts, about *TODAY*'s editorial approach. I knew I had to counter this fresh attack quickly. I went to see David Lim with a thick file containing ST's reports on the region which mixed comment and analysis with news. I remember him telling me: "Balji, don't worry. I know the game that is being played."

The serious editorial bent of our newspaper took SPH by surprise. They had counted on *TODAY* being packed with western-style tabloid fodder, heavy on scandal and female cleavage. Our editorial ideology was just the opposite: *TODAY* emphasised serious stories told in a lively and contextual way. Unlike ST, we went beyond the news, working the background and perspectives into the news, thus providing a meaningful read. As a pre-emptive strike, SPH had launched its own free daily, *Streats*, in September 2000, two months before *TODAY*'s appearance. *Streats*' slogan, "Treats For The Streets", turned out to be a complete miscalculation because it branded them as a downmarket publication, while we were carving out a new market for *TODAY* as a serious tabloid. *Streats*' five or more editorial revamps after *TODAY* launched showed how it struggled to change course in midstream, but the die had been cast and the market had already passed judgement.

Streats had an even bigger battle – an internal one – to fight. It had to play second fiddle to ST and was not allowed to cannibalise the content of the flagship, which provided the bulk of the revenue to SPH's coffers. *TODAY* had no such baggage. All we wanted was 10 per cent of ST's advertising revenue and we would be home and dry. SPH's Cheong Yip Seng, then editor-in-chief of its English and Malay newspapers, was against CEO Tjong Yik Min's plan to introduce *Streats* as a spoiler. Tjong's thinking was that *Streats* would distract *TODAY*, thus giving ST more room to continue to rule the roost. Cheong did not believe ST needed cover and did not want anything to do with *Streats*; thus the freesheet's editor, Ken Jalleh, reported to SPH's marketing chief, Tham Khai Wor. As word got out about the internal dissension in SPH, *Streats* began to lose its confidence.

Both *Streats* and *TODAY* started gunning for advertising dollars from the word go as that was the single tangible factor that would make the difference between success and failure. With both papers being given away free, the only source of revenue was advertising dollars. It helped that I was both editor-in-chief and CEO as I could provide advertisers and advertising agencies solutions no other paper could offer. Hewlett Packard wanted a one-day total buyout of the paper – a monopoly of all the ad spaces – and had their wish granted. Gillette wanted to launch their upside down shaver on Page One with an unusual request: the front page had to be upside down. Again, they got what they wanted.

TODAY's COO Philip Koh and his sales team, with the editorial people right behind them, became a talking point. Of course, the early days were not plain sailing. Senior sales manager, Harry Tan, said:

> The greatest challenge at the time for our marketing team was that advertisers, especially the big ones, were generally afraid to advertise

in *TODAY* because they said they did not want to "burn the bridges" with SPH. These were the exact words uttered by the chairmen and managing directors of companies and advertising agencies that I met. SPH hounded agencies so much so that small and medium-sized agencies were afraid to recommend *TODAY* to their clients, much as they wanted to.

Philip and I went on a counter offensive, telling advertisers and ad agencies what our paper could bring to the table. As we did our rounds explaining *TODAY*'s offerings and its creative ideas, we could see the glint in the eyes of potential clients. A big hit was a never-before-tried solution: wraparound advertisements. Advertisers began to lap them up. After criticising *TODAY* for selling its editorial soul, ST had to surrender and follow suit.

Harry recollects those days with pride: "We were like the flamboyant suitor going around charming advertisers and telling them to let us woo them – and asking for just a fraction of their total budget – so that SPH would sit up and pay them attention. Those days were fun!"

Daisy Chia was one of many sales managers who tweaked conventional approaches to get clients to advertise. She said:

> Our creativity and ideas appealed to art directors in ad agencies. We won accolades with our flexibility to accept different creatives. One of the first advertisers who jumped at the idea was KFC with its pop-up ads. Then there was the large *hongbao* ad from HSBC bank. We also had a special rose-scented edition.

There was, however, some disquiet on the editorial floor about these ads, especially the wraparound ones, as some journalists felt that their stories were being hidden by these ads and that such ads would affect *TODAY*'s editorial reputation. I was in two minds when COO Philip first approached with the idea, so I decided to see for myself the habits of the readers who picked up the paper from the yellow stand placed strategically in MRT stations. It was a revelation. They walked to the stand, picked up the free paper without looking at what was inside and rushed off. They just wanted to read a newspaper on their way to work in the train. Our Page One was the yellow stand and it told me that the free newspaper revolution in Singapore had started.

In *TODAY*'s seamless office, the sales and marketing staff were seated alongside reporters and editors, deleting the traditional gulf between those who produced the newspaper and those who sold it. I had a hunch that clients loved the presence of journalists at meetings. I was proven right as negotiations for contracts became smoother when journalists went along with salespeople. A senior editor could make editorial decisions needed to support the sales team in their marketing efforts and act as a check and balance against over-enthusiasm. Importantly, decisions could be made on the spot.

It worked well, and we were soon producing various supplements with targeted circulation at trade exhibitions. Collin Low, the senior sales manager supporting the travel sector, said:

> Those were the good old days. It honed our ability to become better salespeople, being able to think out of the box and provide intelligent customer service to clients. The team was small but strong. We worked very hard, for example, for the quarterly NATAS travel supplements. It was so gratifying to see the number of pages growing every year!

In support of Collin's efforts, deputy editor Pauline Loh became a prolific travel writer, specialising in Australia and China, two of our largest travel clients.

An important breakthrough brought in major food brands like Lam Soon and Nestlé, and supermarket chains Cold Storage, Carrefour and NTUC FairPrice. Instead of persuading them to buy individual advertisements, the team created a master contract for each client, combining hard and soft sell, which included branding advertisements and sponsored food and recipe pages.

Pauline, a foodie, said: "I remember we convinced the first of them – French hypermarket chain Carrefour – to come in with us because I did a recipe of a pear and chocolate tart, and they sold out on the featured products." Food pages became a major feature in *TODAY*, and at its peak, there was a full page on food every other day.

Editorially, *TODAY* pushed for reports that didn't toe the official line. Empathetic interviews with Opposition leaders, including JB Jeyaretnam, Sylvia Lim and Chiam See Tong, were splashed across Page One. JBJ's interview by Lee Ching Wern was especially striking, with one SPH editor describing it as an "indelible, incandescent story". Headlined "The Lonely Fighter", it told readers how he had "lost everything" and was reduced to living in a room in Oxford Hotel on Queen Street.

Then there were the exclusives, such as the exposé of National Neuroscience Institute director, Professor Simon Shorvon, for taking blood samples from patients without first telling them the samples were for research, a clear breach of medical ethics. And a scoop stolen from right under ST's nose of the navy ship RSS Courageous' collision in 2003 with a merchant ship off Pedra Branca, which killed four people. Scoop specialist Jose Raymond was behind those stories. I was worried about the Courageous exclusive. It had the warning signs of *The New Paper*'s Super Puma crash story all over it. Jose reported precise details of when, how and where it happened, the number of fatalities and identified the ship it had collided with. Having learnt from the Super Puma episode just how hard Mindef could come down on the media, we fudged the details in our report (see Chapter 3).

Deputy editor Rahul Pathak ran the engine room of the editorial department, overseeing a group of bright, energetic – and raw – reporters, all raring to go. Rahul worked his magic by shaping their enthusiastic reporting into highly-readable stories. There was, however, a gaping hole in our early coverage. As readers and advertisers were quick to point out, *TODAY*'s coverage of business and the economy was meagre, especially so for a country that depended so much on these driving forces. That was when former *Business Times* editor, Mano Sabnani, came knocking on our door. He offered to plug that gap by writing for us and training our reporters in business journalism. We shook hands and that started his long relationship with *TODAY*. When I declined to extend my three-year contract in 2003, Mano took over as editor-in-chief.

Mediacorp management was also out there fighting for *TODAY*. Group CEO Ernest Wong rolled up his sleeves and went into the trenches with us. His former role as United Overseas Bank's group president and his close connections with government helped as he used his contacts to raise *TODAY*'s profile and inform the establishment of SPH's tactics. He made a point of attending our management meetings every Tuesday.

When Kwa Chong Seng, chairman and managing director of Exxonmobil Asia Pacific Pte Ltd, was made chairman of

Mediacorp in April 2002, he too joined our Tuesday meetings. It was during one of these meetings in 2002 when he showed his exasperation at *TODAY* for taking a long time to go into the black. I was taken aback. His words, said in front of our management team, who were already under pressure fighting a woken giant, were not what they wanted to hear, especially coming from the chairman.

I told him: "You are the chairman. You have the right and the might to close the paper down." A hush fell on the meeting room, with Ernest Wong stepping in to cool temperatures.

On another occasion, during a Mediacorp board meeting, I asked Kwa Chong Seng if there was any truth to market talk that he and SPH chairman, Lim Kim San, had discussed ending the competition and arranging a merger between the media companies. I had also heard, I said, that Mediacorp was prepared to sacrifice *TODAY* in return for SPH closing down both its TV channels. Competition was getting bloody and both sides were losing money, lots of it. Kwa Chong Seng was candid. He responded with just one word: "Yes." I responded sharply: "So *TODAY* is a guinea pig? How come the *TODAY* team was not told that its future was being dictated like this?" Again, Ernest Wong stepped in – to douse what could have been a heated debate – by saying that talks were informal and exploratory.

In May 2001, about six months into *TODAY*'s launch, I got a call from Mediacorp's corporate office saying that Temasek Holdings' top management team wanted to be briefed by the various business units on their performance and plans. *TODAY* had to give a briefing, too. I thought a 30-minute session would be sufficient. When told that Temasek had requested a longer briefing, I knew it would be a crucial session for the paper.

Mediacorp was a Temasek-linked company and its interest in *TODAY* was understandable. Philip and I realised that what we showed them would be critical to the paper's future. We discussed at length how we should angle the presentation. Should we relate how SPH was blocking us all the way? No, that would sound too defensive. Should we showcase the editorial stance that differentiated *TODAY* from ST? No, they wouldn't be interested. Finally, we decided to just talk business with them; we would analyse our performance to date and map our path forward.

We pored over the daily financial reports that showed the profit-and-loss picture. It was then that we noticed a light shining on us, albeit a small one. We saw that we were making a small profit every Friday; Thursday's edition was also headed towards the black. We had a story – not a great one, but still a story – to tell. If we could make money on Fridays and do reasonably well on Thursdays, then there had to be hope for the other publication days as well. Armed with these statistics, we structured a presentation with this headline: "Is there light at the end of the tunnel?" Our conclusion: yes, there was a light, a flickering one, not that of an on-rushing train.

The Temasek board was a high-powered one chaired by former Cabinet minister, S Dhanabalan. At the time, its members included then Finance Minister Lee Hsien Loong, Permanent Secretary Sim Kee Boon; Minister Lim Hng Khiang and Ho Ching, who would later become CEO of Temasek Holdings. Philip and I knew we had crossed one more bridge on the long road to success when Dhanabalan, who had been chairman of Temasek since September 1996, said: "Oh, this is not the story we have heard."

Bit by bit, the *TODAY* staff began to get their act together. Slowly but steadily, the revenue picture improved. My three-year contract was coming to an end and the paper was inching towards breakeven status. It was left to Mano Sabnani, who took over from me, to make it profitable. That was achieved two years later in 2005.

CHAPTER 10

Last of the Mohicans
Why the editors of old did it differently

When former editor-in-chief of *The Straits Times*, Cheong Yip Seng, launched his book, *OB Markers: My Straits Times Story*,[1] in October 2012, an unexpected and pointed question was lobbed at him: Will your book get you into trouble?

The question came from ST Opinion editor, Chua Mui Hoong. The extent and nature of the disclosures in the memoir had surprised even some old hands. This was the first time an editor of Cheong Yip Seng's stature and longevity – 43 years in journalism, nearly 20 as editor-in-chief – had put on record the Singapore government's moves to control and shape the national narrative through media reports, as well as the few occasions when editors had resisted Lee Kuan Yew's instructions.

Like a *taiji* master trying to avoid an inconvenient interference, Cheong's reply to her was cryptic: "There is a guardian angel protecting me." Was he referring to God … or to Lee Kuan Yew? No one followed up on this during the panel discussion held in connection with the launch, but the question was decidedly prescient.

---

[1] Cheong Yip Seng, *OB Markers: My Straits Times Story* (Straits Times Press, 2012).

The government's reaction to the book came surreptitiously and without any public statement. Cheong's appointment as non-resident Ambassador to Chile in 2010 was not renewed when it ended three years later; more tellingly, when *OB Markers* was reprinted, Lee Kuan Yew's endorsement disappeared from the book. The government was unhappy that one of its most trusted journalists had embarrassed it so publicly. This was, after all, *The Straits Times'* (ST) longest-surviving editor-in-chief – he had lasted a few months short of 20 years. The official mythology had always been that the government did not interfere in the media. So trusted was Cheong that no one in government had even asked to look over his manuscript.

Cheong was a political animal, giving in to demands when he knew fighting the government was hopeless, and that staying alive to fight another day was a better and safer option. He sewed up the political ground by winning Lee Kuan Yew's confidence, giving hardly any reason for the strongman to be displeased with his leadership of the newsroom. He knew he had to manage the newsroom to make sure that sensitive stories were written with the right angles and tone. To achieve that, he had to be completely clued in to Lee's thinking and also to newsroom personalities and operations. What he gleaned from informal meetings with Lee and other ministers, he used to get a deeper understanding of government thinking on local and foreign issues. He was so familiar with the nitty-gritty of newsroom operations that he knew exactly when to intervene and who to call. He would check on stories from home and telephone the right people in the newsroom to get changes made.

His antenna was at its most sensitive when monitoring election stories. When the People's Action Party (PAP) lost one more seat in the general election of 1984, making it two in a row after JB Jeyaretnam and his Workers' Party cracked the PAP's monopoly in 1981, Cheong chose a headline for *The Sunday Times* story that made many in the newsroom cringe: "PAP wins all but two". Its rival, *The Sunday Monitor*, went with "Jeya and Chiam win". Neither headline could be faulted as they were both factual and accurate, but *The Sunday Times* headline did not underline the political significance as much as *The Sunday Monitor*'s did. That *The Sunday Times* came across as pro-PAP and *The Sunday Monitor* as a better reflection of the news significance was not lost on observers, who saw the loss of another seat as a big deal in a country where a single party had monopolised Parliament for so long. Four years later, when former Solicitor-General-turned-government-critic Francis Seow electrified the 1988 contest as an Opposition candidate, Cheong was told to douse the political excitement inflaming the country. Accordingly, the following day's coverage in ST was considerably reduced.

There is another side to Cheong that hardly comes up for discussion: he is the consummate newsman. He knew the news business inside out, having clawed his way up from reporter to chief reporter, news editor, editor and, finally, editor-in-chief. When he was news editor of ST, he would show up for work on Saturday, his day off, to pick up sub-editing skills. He would dive into newspapers from around the world, studying how they reported events. In the early 1980s, I was night editor of ST when Cheong was already the paper's editor. From my vantage position on the night desk, I observed how he shaped stories with a sharp eye and an even sharper pen. It was a great learning experience. I saw how he masterminded coverage of one of the most dramatic and sensational stories of our time:

the downing of Korean Airlines Flight 007 from New York to Seoul via Anchorage by a Soviet Union SU-15 Interceptor on 1 September 1983. The Soviets claimed that the passenger craft was on a spying mission. It was actually on a scheduled flight from New York to Seoul and had apparently entered Soviet airspace. The in-house wordsmith, Peter Barnard, was assigned to head a team of writers whom Cheong himself briefed on every possible angle of a story that would shake the world. The excitement in the editor's voice and face was evident for all to see. It wasn't just spectacular foreign news breaks that seized his imagination. When reports surfaced of people flinging furniture and heavy household objects from high-rise flats, Cheong had ST launch a campaign against such anti-social behaviour, and coined the term "killer litter" to describe the menace, a term that has become a fixture in the Singapore lexicon.

Former ST journalist, Cherian George, a Hong Kong-based academic, highlighted a third side to Cheong Yip Seng's leadership. In a 2018 book by Simon Vincent, *The Naysayers Book Club*, Cherian observed that ST editors "were very good at protecting their staff".[2] He told Vincent:

> The editor-in-chief at that time, Cheong Yip Seng, saw his role as being the buffer between the press and the government. At that time (in the early 1990s), I was very critical of him ... he's very pro-PAP, very conservative. It's only on hindsight that you realise that he played this very important role. He wouldn't sell any staff down the river.

---

[2] Simon Vincent, *The Naysayers Book Club: 26 Singaporeans you need to know* (Epigram Books, 2018).

Cheong Yip Seng was able to do this "very delicate dance" of managing the government's expectations, said Cherian, and for a man capable of performing such a delicate dance, it was a surprise that he wrote a book like *OB Markers*. The government was not happy, of course. Lee Kuan Yew's daughter, Lee Wei Ling, wrote on her blog post that Prime Minister Lee Hsien Loong had "scolded" Cheong on the phone. She had called Cheong to tell him that her father was not upset about the contents of his book. "Your father is too big for this ... (he) did not scold me. He wanted to point out some issues. I tried to explain to Hsien Loong that I was defending your father, not attacking him," she quoted Cheong as telling her. It is still a mystery why Cheong wrote that book. My only explanation is that he wanted to leave journalism with a bang, and he did not want to leave behind a legacy of being known as a government lackey.

There is another view, articulated by a media watcher:

> Cheong genuinely believed that being pro-government was nothing to be ashamed of. I read his book as a reminder to new ministers and new editors that the relationship was a special and delicate one needing mutual respect. That is why he gave some examples of the difficult negotiations and the give-and-take with the government. He feared that it was becoming a more one-way subservient relationship.

Peter Lim, Cheong's predecessor at ST, had hardly an easy relationship with Lee Kuan Yew. In fact, it was rocky most times. Not that Peter was a strident critic of the Lee Kuan Yew government. I have heard him give a very balanced view of the man many times, speaking highly of his intellect and achievements. Peter's fatal flaw, in Lee Kuan Yew's eyes, was in believing that the media should be given room to dissent occasionally. Case in point: when Lee wanted the full "O" Level results of PAP candidate Mah Bow Tan and his rival, Chiam See Tong, reported in ST. The year was 1984; Chiam See Tong and the Singapore Democratic Party he founded in 1980 were standing against PAP's new find, Mah Bow Tan, in Potong Pasir. Lee Kuan Yew said at an election rally: "Mah Bow Tan, age 16, took his "O" levels – six distinctions, two credits. Mr Chiam, age 18, six credits, one pass."

Afterwards, Lee's press secretary, James Fu, telephoned Peter to say that the PM wanted the detailed examination scores of every subject the two men had taken to be published in ST. Peter replied respectfully that if the PM had disclosed the full exam results during the rally, ST would use it in its report. But the PM had not, so using the information in a report would not be good for the government and ST. The rumour mill would go into overdrive and people would speculate that the details had been deliberately leaked to ST, he said. James Fu telephoned several more times, trying to persuade Peter to change his mind. The editor-in-chief stood firm and, in the end, Lee Kuan Yew did not get his way.

Peter's bravest moment of resistance came when Ong Teng Cheong, then Communications Minister, took the extraordinary step of holding a high-level press conference to excoriate ST and *New Nation* publicly for a source-based story on impending bus fare hikes. As acting editor of *New Nation*, I was present with Peter and other editors at the press conference. When asked to name the source or sources for the reports, he declined, explaining that it ran counter to journalism ethics. The to-ing and fro-ing between minister and editor was there for all to read in the next day's paper. See Chapter 3 for more details.

Yet another instance of Peter's independence was his pushback of Lee's plan to get the Singapore media to emulate Japan's cosy press-government relationship. At its core were the infamously cosy "press clubs", whose members were physically based in the different ministries. The clubs controlled access to government information and thus limited the reporting that checked government wrongdoings. The result: reporters becoming pally with civil servants and ministers, blurring the lines between journalists and official power brokers. A major flaw in this approach: "The convenient access to information and the relations with authorities may discourage reporters at the press clubs from carrying out investigative reporting," said *The Japan Times*.[3] Peter felt that the existing government-media arrangement in Singapore, including informal access to official thinking on policies and the strict press laws, were sufficient. For reasons unknown, Lee Kuan Yew did not pursue the plan.

That arrangement, however, failed to prevent two reports filed by Peter from Brunei from becoming problematic. Both covered an official visit to Brunei, one of Singapore's closest neighbours. In an ST report of 21 August 1986, Peter Lim wrote that Brigadier-General (Ret) Lee Hsien Loong, Lee Kuan Yew's son, had missed the target during a shooting practice. Lee Kuan Yew had fired first and his shot had come near the target. He then turned to his son and said: "Have a go, Loong. Let's see whether you use less (bullets)." The Brigadier-General missed the target

---

[3] Kanako Takahara, "Press clubs: Exclusive access to, pipelines for info" *The Japan Times*, 30 January 2007 <https://www.japantimes.co.jp/news/2007/01/30/reference/press-clubs-exclusive-access-to-pipelines-for-info/#.XIomBWaB0UQ>

altogether. Afterwards, Lee Senior said, teasingly, to his son: "It looks as if you're a bad marksman." The son was then Acting Minister of Trade and Industry and Acting Minister of Defence. Peter recorded all this in his report headlined "A day of choppers, fire power petro-links, family tea and dinner talk". So far, not so bad.

Two days later, however, he delivered a follow-up report with this unusual headline: "Rashomon on the firing range – Was it a hit or a miss for the general with the gun?" The commander of the Singapore Armed Forces' Brunei training base, Lieutenant-Colonel Malcolm Alphonso, was quoted as saying, "He did NOT miss," as Lee Hsien Loong was firing at the brick targets behind the electronic pop-up targets. Not satisfied, Peter asked why the acting minister had not shot at the life-sized pop-up targets. "Because they are too simple for him," Lieutenant-Colonel Alphonso said. In his effort to chase the complete story, Peter quoted an unnamed person as saying: "The bullets hit the bricks because they missed the target and went astray."

Lieutenant-Colonel Alphonso told Peter that his first report did the visiting minister a disservice. Peter decided to check with the man himself. Lee Hsien Loong's reply: "It is not important. Just forget it." As any good reporter would do, Peter pressed: "Did I do you a disservice?" Again the reply was the same: "Just forget it." Not satisfied, Peter asked another question: "Did you aim for the pop-ups or the bricks?" "The bricks," came the reply. "Then I owe you an apology." Again, the reply was the same: "Just forget it."

Peter concluded his follow-up with an unexpected ending: "Now, don't the different impressions remind you of the classic Japanese film, *Rashomon*? A samurai was murdered and his wife raped by a bandit. The court heard three versions of the same event. The filmgoer sees a fourth. I feel like the woodcutter in the film. I came by, I saw, but I did not see it all."

That 1950 film, a psychological thriller that delves into the nature of truth and the meaning of justice, was much discussed and dissected in newspaper reports and academic journals when it was released. Canadian academic Robert Anderson wrote: "The Rashomon effect is not only about differences in perspective. It occurs particularly where such differences arise in combination with absence of evidence to elevate or disqualify any version of the truth ..."[4] In short, THE truth is hard to get at. Only shades of THE truth are available.

So, what was Peter trying to do in that controversial follow-up report? To show up the Brigadier-General's marksmanship? In the more than 40 years I have known Peter, not once have I seen him embarrass anyone, let alone a politician. Was he trying to be cheeky? Again, no. He took his profession seriously; he was never cheeky in official or unofficial dealings with politicians, colleagues and friends. Was he so intent on lightening his serious political coverage from Brunei that he forgot or ignored how that "Rashomon report" could affect the image of the Prime Minister's son, a fast-riser in the Cabinet and a former military man at that? That is the only plausible explanation I can think of. Also – and here is where Peter Lim's independent streak comes in – that incident happened at an event open to press coverage. Many would have seen it, and had he failed to record it, that would

---

[4] Robert Anderson, "The Rashomon Effect and Communication" *Canadian Journal of Communication* Vol 41, No 2 (2016) 249–269 at 265.

have been interpreted as self-censorship. However, could he have done it without linking it to *Rashomon*? Only Peter can answer that. I hope he will fill in that gap one day. His last paragraph – or kicker, as it is known in journalistic lingo – left the story with no real conclusion, only doubt. And doubt tends to raise suspicion, especially in a government inclined to regard journalists with a jaundiced eye.

Peter's management style was very different from that of his predecessors. He was a listener, always ready to hear out his journalists when they approached him. He ran an open and transparent newsroom and believed in the principle that government and media should not be one. There should be a line, no matter how thin, between the two. He believed the PAP was good for Singapore, but not that all its actions were correct. In his eight years as editor-in-chief of ST, that streak of independence would always land him in trouble.

Peter was an ST evangelist. As editor-in-chief, he preached incessantly about making the paper more readable. He held an unprecedented series of newsroom-wide seminars, despite many journalists' scepticism, to explain what he meant and what would happen if ST continued to follow the tried-and-tested path of writing reports about ministers' speeches and official policies (ST's readership would decline over time). That was in the 1980s when the paper was in a commanding and formidable position, with no immediate threats to its continued success visible.

Peter was also a visionary; he wanted to prepare for the "what-if" scenario. The reports from Brunei were his attempt to lead by example, and show the journalists what he meant by a light touch. He had always believed in hooking the reader with a touch of the unexpected. He had to have thought the off-target shots by Lee Hsien Loong added a human interest dimension to the weightier reports on Brunei-Singapore relations. These and other testy episodes, such as his public tussle with then Communications Minister Ong Teng Cheong, meant that his days leading the newsroom were numbered.

A retired journalist who had survived those tumultuous years in ST recounted: "It was one crisis after another in Times House. Peter would hold meetings with staff to explain the background to each crisis. Until the inevitable happened."

That came on 31 December 1986, when a report in ST announced Peter's resignation and said he would take over as "chief editor" of a new newspaper, *The New Paper*, to be launched by SPH. "Mr Lim, with his nearly 30 years of newspaper experience, has all the attributes to lead and launch the project successfully," SPH said in an announcement that left much unsaid. It neither said, for instance, that Cheong Yip Seng had been originally entrusted with the new project, nor gave a reason for it being handed over to Peter. The decision to replace Peter had been made some time before that. Cheong revealed in his book that Goh Chok Tong had told him during a flight back home from Myanmar in December about a year before that he wanted him to take over as editor-in-chief.

Even without that sliver of a revelation, many in the newsroom knew that Peter was paying a price for his belief that media should not be totally subservient to government. There was also a belief in government circles that Peter was too liberal in the way he dealt with staff. In short, he didn't want to control the newsroom with a firm hand – which was what the government had wanted.

Peter never uttered a word about why he was leaving, except for a cryptic one-liner he gave to historian Mary Turnbull in her book commissioned by ST for its 150th anniversary. In that book, *Dateline Singapore: 150 years of the Straits Times*, he says: "The board told me my deputy was ready to take over."[5]

Hidden in that quote was a message that could be read thousands of miles away. Peter was then a youthful 48 and had been in the top editorial job for only eight years. So why was there a need to ask him to step down at that time? His deputy was 44 and could have easily waited a few more years to take over. Goh Chok Tong became Prime Minister a mere four years later in 1990. Even if Goh Chok Tong had wanted a new editor-in-chief with whom he was comfortable, he could have waited.

As the newsrooms grappled with these issues, Peter convened a meeting for journalists of all the newspapers under his watch. It was a long and emotional townhall-style gathering, with Peter trying to answer all the questions thrown at him.

In response to one question, he dropped this bombshell: "I give Cheong a 50-50 chance of success." This was not the Peter Lim with whom so many of us were familiar – dignified and embracing. And, for sure, this was no ringing endorsement of the man taking over from him. Moreover, it seemed entirely uncharacteristic of Peter, who had already made it known earlier that he wanted his deputy to succeed him but likely at a time of his own choosing.

Three years later, just before Peter left SPH in 1990, he wrote a note to Cheong Yip Seng that he copied to senior editors, taking

---

[5] Constance Mary Turnbull, *Dateline Singapore: 150 years of the Straits Times* (Times Editions, 1995).

back that "50-50 chance of success" prediction he had made at the meeting, and ending his note with "I salute you".

Leslie Fong stepped into Cheong Yip Seng's shoes as editor of ST with Peter Lim's sense of mission to keep ST from becoming a government mouthpiece. Unlike his predecessor, Leslie stamped his editorship with a commitment to show his staff that every story, even stories that were politically sensitive, could be published if care and subtlety were applied. Soon, Leslie found himself getting into a tangle with officialdom. His public defence of Sumiko Tan in 1991 over her commentary criticising a Member of Parliament's statement revealed what was on the horizon.[6] In a private setting, Leslie and Minister for Information and the Arts George Yeo engaged in a debate over the issue, with George Yeo finally declaring that the government would defend its Members of Parliament even if they were wrong. Leslie's rejoinder was a brave admission of reality: "We know our blood will be on the floor." Then came Lee Kuan Yew's reaction to several of Leslie's commentaries in his column "Thinking Aloud". Lee wanted him sacked. SPH executive chairman Lim Kim San worked out a deal that would keep him as editor, but in a non-writing role. An emotionless Leslie told editors: "Chairman saved my ass."

The writing, however, was on the wall, and when it came time for Cheong Yip Seng to retire, it was not Leslie, but Patrick Daniel, then managing editor, who took over as editor-in-chief. Leslie, who was fluent in Chinese and had once been editor of *Shin Min Daily News*, was moved to take charge of ST's China coverage, while Han Fook Kwang became ST editor.

---

[6] See Chapter 3.

Leslie's relationship with Cheong Yip Seng had never been easy. While the latter believed in skirting open warfare with government and living to fight another day, Leslie was different. When calls came from officialdom, he would hear them out, giving in when he thought the request was fair but pushing back when he disagreed. Soon, officials learnt to bypass him and approach Cheong directly, which irritated Leslie to no end. Leslie also had strong views about what ST's content should be, and wanted the paper to tackle the serious local and international issues of the day, while playing down human interest stories. He also wanted its look and feel to be that of a serious paper. He initially refused, for instance, to allow colour pictures except for important occasions such as National Day, but he soon had to give in, persuaded by his deputies that the newspaper world was changing. Similarly, he was not in favour of a redesign of ST by American designer Roger Black, but Cheong had secured the approval of senior management and Leslie had no choice but to go along. There was no open hostility between them, but their disagreements were palpable, especially during meetings with senior editors.

Leslie was known – even feared – in the newsroom for his Grammar Nazi absolutism towards language. In his book, Singaporeans of Chinese descent were never to be described as Singaporean Chinese, but as Chinese Singaporeans. The same linguistic logic applied to Singaporeans of other ethnic origins. Any transgression might result in an editorial explosion. He was a stickler for discipline, ordering his staff to be dressed properly, especially for press conferences and interviews. "You are an ST employee, keep that in mind," he would chide those spotted dressed sloppily. That earned him such labels as Attila the Hun, dictator, bully and despot. There were, however, chinks in his armour. He had a soft spot for many staff, especially those who had entered the profession with him as reporters. When they had to retire, he often managed to find part-time jobs for those who wanted or needed them.

These three newsroom leaders – Cheong Yip Seng, Peter Lim and Leslie Fong – and many others of their generation were journalism's "Last of the Mohicans". They grew into the profession in an era when colonial influence ran deep and strong. Nearly every English-language journalist in the Singapore of that era began by looking to Fleet Street for inspiration and excitement. British journalism books such as *The Simple Subs Book* by Leslie Sellers,[7] *Newspaper Design* by Harold Evans[8] and *Cassandra: reflections in the mirror* by Robert Connor[9] became the reading mantra.

I asked academic and former ST journalist, Cherian George, why that generation of journalists did what they did. He said:

> I would put it in one word: Culture. Newsroom. Professional. Your generation was socialised into journalism before PAP stamped its own culture on the press from the 1980s. These editors didn't face a kinder, gentler government. But they grew up in journalism with a stronger sense that the press was not part of the establishment. My generation benefited from having supervisors who had that instinct. Even if your decisions were ultimately constrained, we could see

---

[7] Leslie Sellers, *The Simple Subs Book* (Pergamon Press, November 1968).
[8] Harold Evans, *Newspaper Design – An Illustrated Guide to Layout* (Heinemann, 1973).
[9] Robert Connor, *Cassandra: reflections in the mirror* (Cassell, 1969)

day to day that you all valued whatever independence you were able to carve out. It was something precious and you all didn't take it lightly. In the 1990s culture, with you guys in charge, there was also plenty of back and forth of ideas in the newsroom. Even as a rookie reporter, I felt I could speak my mind in the newsroom. Ultimately, the product was largely conservative and pro-government, but I felt the newsroom was still a fun and stimulating place because of that open and professional atmosphere. When your generation retired, the press lost that connection to the pre-consolidation era.

You may have noticed that I have been silent on the generation of journalists running the print media today. That silence is deliberate. In the 1970s, 1980s and 1990s, I was an active participant in newsroom decision-making and had a firsthand view of the conundrums and conflicts that the editors of that era experienced with officialdom. At the time of writing this book, I am already a distant observer and not clued-in to how today's editors think, act and reflect. Journalism has evolved into a very different creature, facing very different challenges. It is a story that has to be left to a whole new generation of journalists to write.

ANNEX

I have selected ten published articles to reflect my thinking on some of the issues that have occupied my mind over the years. Two of these articles were not written by me: one was an interview I gave to a bright NTU student and the other a public conversation with academic Cherian George. The issues raised in these articles are still relevant today and I am pleased I wrote about them. One article was from a personal column and that was about my grandson, Arrian. Three years later, I see a different boy, one who is confident and caring. I hope he will continue on this path.

1. THE VETERAN

What is the future of journalism in Singapore? Even after helming three of Singapore's largest English dailies, PN Balji has no answers on the future of newspapers, only ideas.

by Sheere Ng

This article was first published on the website "Where are we going?" in early 2009 and posted on justinzhuang.com on 20 June 2009.

Standing in front of a room filled with seasoned journalists and students, P.N. Balji is incredibly at ease. He leans against the table and props one leg over the edge, revealing his bare ankle and grey suede shoes – just like his suggestions, his sense of style is incredibly wayward.

At a time when newspapers are dying, the director of the Asia Journalism Fellowship is here to talk about the future of journalism. He challenges his audience about the possibilities of a borderless newspaper- one with no clear delineated sections.

Why not let movie reviews appear on the front page? The International Herald Tribune did that with The Dark Knight. How about running the piece on former US secretary of state Madeleine Albright's jewellery in the prime pages instead of burying it in the lifestyle section? "It's a fantastic article about how she communicates her mood through the brooches she wears. It is politics, fashion, and personal profile," he says. "At the end of the day, readers just want to read a good story."

Although he provides no solution to the newspaper crisis and instead chooses to raise numerous questions that set the room thinking, his journalistic journey may shed some light. After all, the 60-year-old has spent half his life working in The Straits Times (ST), The New Paper (TNP) and Today.

Newsroom chameleon

In 1988, Balji left his job as ST's deputy editor to join the pioneering team of TNP.

At that time there was a vacuum in the marketplace for fresh news to provide different insights. Balji's team thus launched a tabloid paper that attracted a new group of readers: they are young, they did not read newspapers before, and they only read TNP.

But the man himself is not big on tabloid sensationalism.

"That doesn't mean I can't produce it," he says. "You must divorce yourself from what you like, to give the market what it likes." Journalists cannot afford to listen only to themselves as they have vested interests and biases, he adds.

Some 12 years later, with ST aiming squarely at the entire English-speaking public, TNP providing tabloid news and Streats, a free commuter tabloid sheet, it just didn't seem there was a market for another.

"So we created one," he says. In 2000, Balji joined MediaCorp to set up Today, another commuter tabloid sheet. "We decided that the newspaper should provide news that is 'not overtly pro-government' and will tackle issues that The Straits Times will shy away from."

Today, Singapore's media landscape looks set to change again. In the US, the mainstream media is wilting under the onslaught of online journalism and Web 2.0. Advertising looks set to shift its operations to capture more of the online audience and demand for print advertising is falling fast.

According to Jeffrey Seah, CEO of Starcom Media Group, a leading multinational advertising company, being able to engage users gives the Internet an important edge over mainstream media in selling advertising space.

Newspapers like ST, on other hand, are facing an uphill task of retaining their audience. With more news sources available on the internet, the public's reading habits are changing even more quickly. One example would be Balji himself.

According to him, he used to receive the bulk of his information from traditional print media a few months ago. Today, 60 per cent of his information comes from the internet.

He has been relying on the 'pushing' of information online by his friends who will forward him any interesting news nuggets they come across. "I do follow blogs like The Online Citizen and Yawning Bread," says Balji. "But if I start to read news websites like ST Online or CNA (Channelnewsasia), then I will have no time to sleep."

But his time is not only spent online. His practice of journalism seeps into his everyday life as well.

Pedestrian tasks like grocery shopping and visits to the petrol stations take unusually long for Balji as he tries to take the time to talk to anyone who might come along. "All these little bits of information will hopefully give you the ground feel of what people like and don't like over time," he says.

But Balji hasn't always been this comfortable talking to strangers. He describes himself as "very much an introvert who is trying very hard to be an extrovert".

Reminiscing, he recalls that his interest in journalism began when he was young. He remembers having to get up as early as possible before his father and younger brother in order to read the family's only copy of ST in peace. At that time, he was a firm devotee of Norman Siebel's (former Straits Times Sports Editor) articles.

From fighting for to fighting with The Straits Times

But as he grew older, his relationship with Singapore Press Holdings (SPH) was no longer as filled with bliss. This was because he joined MediaCorp to help launch Today, today seen as a direct competitor to ST.

"Some people might think I'm a traitor," he admits. But Balji sticks by his philosophy- to "go when the going is good". Leaving while you are at the top of your game puts your life in your own hands rather than your employer's, he explains.

This was also why he left TNP earlier on, when the paper was at its dizzying heights. From a circulation of 50, 000, it hit a ceiling of 130, 000 when he left.

Similarly, in 2003, Balji ended his contract with MediaCorp after three years with Today to work in the Public Relations (PR) industry, which some journalism practitioners have dubbed the 'darker side'. He went on to set up two flourishing PR companies – Bang Public Relations and Communications DNA.

"I would have liked to continue in journalism. But where do I go?" he says. Leaving Singapore Press Holdings (SPH) to join its competitor to start Today has left him with little options.

But when he was asked to return to Today in 2007 when its editor-in-chief, Mano Sabnani, left, Balji returned to the fold.

"My first concern was that Today must not go down. Why should we let SPH have the last laugh?" he says. He denies that bad blood exists between him and SPH but merely feels that Singapore journalism can benefit from more competition.

Ironically, it is precisely this lack of competition in the local newspaper industry that may be keeping newspapers here afloat. "If you ask me today: can I throw the Straits Times away? I can't," he says. In the West, there are so many competitors that newspapers are winding up or looking to investors for help after incurring millions of dollars in losses.

In Singapore, the lack of alternative news media has bred mediocrity in the standards and professionalism of local news coverage in the mainstream press. "They are surviving only because readers do not have a benchmark to make comparisons with," says Balji.

Soon after his last contract with Today ended, he tried to set up a full-blown online newspaper like The Huffington Post. But he could not find a viable business model for his publication.

"I only managed to find a cost model, but not a revenue model," he says. Hence, he feels that the prospect of an alternative online newspaper might not be a viable undertaking for now, yet another reason that is keeping newspapers here safe. But Balji estimates that Singapore has only about five to ten years before the full impact of the fundamental shift in the media landscape is felt.

However, tell-tale signs of this change are popping out. Singaporeans increasingly look to the Internet for news that the mainstream media chooses to ignore or to censor. "This is the biggest problem that the mainstream media faces," says Balji.

More of such cases have been seen in recent years. For instance, news of the suicide of a Singapore Armed Forces medical officer first broke on the internet before making its way to the papers. Recently, ST also left out questions about Prime Minister Lee Hsien Loong's pay when it reported an interview he did with the British Broadcasting Corporation (BBC).

"What frustrates Singaporean readers most is that the mainstream media are blocking out news," he says. "But what is important is that now, they can get it online."

Journalists are the greatest enemy of journalism

"The conventional reporting style of "A says this and B says that" no longer satisfy today's media-savvy readers," says Balji during his presentation.

Comparing the two instances when he created TNP and Today to fill the voids in the market, he says that the demand for news analysis has become even greater in recent years, and especially so today.

In the recent terrorist attacks on Mumbai, he had stayed up overnight to follow the breaking news on television. That was why he was very disappointed to see the same information in the newspapers the morning after. "Why would people want to read something they already knew about?" he questions.

Not only that, Balji thinks there is a dearth of stories that provide fresh insights and new viewpoints. For example, no one in the mainstream press had questioned why the PM held a press conference after the recent Cabinet reshuffle. "Nothing like that has ever happened in Singapore's history, but I didn't see any article helping the reader make sense of it," he says.

Some say that the self-preservation and self-censorship are reasons why local journalists choose not to delve deeper into such issues. However, Balji feels that journalists cannot see themselves as ordinary citizens with such ordinary fears. "That's why we go into this profession," he says.

There is also more required of journalists today. Besides writing, they should also be equipped with other skills like photography and newspaper design. "Newsrooms have a tendency to be overstaffed," he says. Especially so in bad times, journalists with multiple skills are more likely to be valued.

When he joined ST as a rookie, he chose editor-in-chief, T.S. Khoo as his mentor. To him, Khoo was the best layout designer in Asia at that time and Balji wanted to learn design from him. Daily, the young Balji picked up dummy sheets of the newspaper layout that Khoo had thrown into the waste paper basket.

Putting all the crumpled sheets beside the final published paper, he saw for himself the evolution of the entire design process. "That was a priceless learning experience," he says

Today's competitive economic climate also calls for journalist to be more aware of the business of news. "A good journalist must know his market well," says Balji. Learning the ropes, he suggests, can be as easy as having lunch with colleagues from the advertising and marketing department. Unfortunately, many journalists today either do not know, or do not want to know about advertising and marketing and cite maintaining 'editorial integrity' as their excuse.

Balji knows that old mindsets cannot be changed in the span of an hour. So he concluded his presentation with a quote by Rupert Murdoch, a man that journalists claim is threatening their credibility, "Journalists are threatening their own papers". A dire warning is sounded by the most unlikely of allies – that if journalists today do not change their mindsets, they are liable to bring journalism down with them.

This story is part of a series, Where are we going: The future of newspapers in Singapore.

Reproduced with permission.

The NTU students dug deep into my personality to bring out traits that I had kind of forgotten.

2. WHAT HAVE WE DONE FOR OUR MERDEKA GENERATION?

by PN Balji

This commentary was first published in *TODAY* on 10 August 2009.

I belong to the Lucky Generation. Born soon after World War II into a tumultuous world, by a twist of good faith and fortune, we became the early beneficiaries of Singapore's economic success.

Three moves catapulted people of my generation out of a Singapore in the backwaters to a Singapore in the ocean of prosperity: the Central Provident Fund (CPF), high salaries and housing.

A young Singaporean recently gasped in awe as I told her that there was a point in our lives when we were forced to save 50 per cent of our monthly salaries, 25 per cent paid by ourselves and the other 25 per cent by our employers. At age 55, for many of us, there was more than a cool million dollars waiting to be collected.

It was about the same time that Mr Lee Kuan Yew and his team decided that Singapore should up the economic game and move into producing high-end goods. That was done by forcing companies to pay their workers higher wages or move their operations out of Singapore.

The result: Those lucky enough not to work in the Singapore sweatshops saw their salaries rise by $1,000 a month. Can you imagine what this kind of extra income, and that too in the early 1980s, could have done to your bottom line and your spirits?

And, finally, housing. Thirty-three years ago, I bought my first home (not house, as today's Singaporeans like to say) for $97,500. Home, sweet home, it provided more than a roof over our heads, appreciating in value many times over. Many profited by buying and selling and then re-buying and re-selling as the country turbocharged its way into an economic never-never land.

Believe it or not, a friend of mine paid a deposit for a town house in Faber Garden and just weeks later sold it for a profit of $100,000 because the property agent had found a willing buyer. That was in 1990.

As my mind goes back to such stories of the Lucky Generation this National Day, I can't help but think of the generation before us, the Merdeka Generation.

The group that gave the People's Action Party(PAP) its biggest break by voting the then opposition party into power in the 1959 elections with a 43-51 majority in Parliament.

Would we have the Singapore that we see today if not for that momentous moment on May 30, 1959? Highly unlikely.

They are now in their 70s, 80s and some even in their 90s. There are an estimated 191,000 of them, some in good health and happily retired, some bedridden, some breaking their backs cleaning up after us in food outlets and even some being pushed in wheelchairs by the maids at some of our parks.

At 8.22pm last night, many of us stopped for a moment to take the Singapore pledge.

It is time to start thinking of another pledge, this time for our Merdeka Generation: We, the citizens of Singapore, pledge to look after our Merdeka Generation by taking care of their needs and wants in a way that they can live their golden years in happiness and look back at the nation they helped to create with joy and pride.

The Government can go one step further by easing one of their biggest fears: Health care. Put aside a bare minimum sum to take care of their health needs?

Is that too much to ask of a nation that might not even be a dot if not for these people?

Reproduced with permission.

This commentary was written four years before the government introduced schemes for the so-called pioneer generation. The package was instrumental in the ruling People's Action Party winning back the votes it lost in 2011.

3. AN OPPORTUNITY MISSED?

What Walter Woon's interview says of change in Singapore

by PN Balji

This commentary was first published in *TODAY* on 19 April 2010.

In Singapore, any exit interview is a slippery business. Leave the scene with guns blazing, like former President Ong Teng Cheong did, and be prepared for a rapid-fire response.

Do it with lips half-sealed, like most Singaporeans do, and expect the rumour mill to go into high gear.

Former Attorney-General Water Woon chose a middle path: Reveal quite a bit but leave a lot to the reader's imagination.

Here's a sampling of his diplomat-lawyer speak: "The longest period in my life".

One can read that statement in many ways. Was he saying that it was the worst or toughest period in his life?

Or, that it was the most challenging?

Asked if he had annoyed the powers that be, Mr Woon's reply was that it was "not unlikely".

Since two negatives make a positive, it must mean that his departure was due to problems he had with people upstairs.

But it leaves enough wiggle room for him to say: I never said that.

There was one quote that betrayed his sentiments very clearly: "I think among some people, I've already overstayed my welcome." Hmmm ... very careful people who know how to twist and turn the language and keep people guessing can sometimes slip and give away some truths.

Mr Woon's departure and his farewell interview, however he tried to shade it, show that the Singapore establishment has some way to go in redefining the line between public and private discourse.

The law academic and former diplomat tried to define it his own way.

He got into a public spat with Dr Lee Wei Ling over whether C K Tang boss Tang Wee Sung should be shown some kind of a mercy because of the retailer's illness. Mr Woon was categorical, and some might say, principled.

He said Mr Tang's lies in a statutory declaration about buying a kidney "was an assault on our basic foundation of law ... You can't lie on oath".

Mr Woon didn't start the public debate. Dr Lee did that with her letter to The Straits Times in 2008. Some other senior civil servant would have got his spokespeople to sign off the response. Not Mr Woon; he put his name to the letter.

Then there was the case in 2008 when he went to court to appeal against the nine-year sentence given to a woman for instigating her boyfriend to kill her husband.

Mr Woon said he argued the appeal personally because the case carried on from when he was Solicitor-General in 2007. Still, unusual by Singapore standards.

He appeared for the Government in another appeal, this time brought by a man given the death sentence for drug trafficking. Mr Woon explained he wanted to defend the constitutionality of Singapore's death penalty. Not really necessary, for it is an old issue and could have been left to a DPP to handle.

There was no doubt that Singaporeans were seeing a very different AG, one who won't shy away from doing what he thought was right, whether in private or in public. The august and rarefied place that the legal fraternity is versus an AG who was just the opposite — a face-off was inevitable.

Mr Woon must have decided that change — the word thrust into the world's consciousness by United States President Barack Obama — is not going to happen the way he envisioned it. So he decided not to extend his two-year contract, not even wanting to wait for his successor Sundaresh Menon to take over from him on Oct 1.

Like in the case of Mr Chip Goodyear, who quit even before he took up his CEO post at Temasek Holdings, somebody forgot to tell Mr Woon that the Singapore culture of top officials articulating their points of view in public is still a no-go.

Like Mr Woon's appointment was a great opportunity to change all that — but it's now gone. That's a pity, really.

Reproduced with permission.

I enjoyed writing this commentary as I dug deep into what then Attorney General Walter Woon said in his farewell interview. Although he tried to shade the true reason for his departure, I said it was clear his departure was not a happy one.

4. WHERE IS THE NEW NORMAL IN SINGAPORE POLITICS?

by PN Balji

This article was first published in Yahoo News on 20 July 2011.

Presidential hopeful Dr Tony Tan will do himself – and Singapore politics – a huge favour if he stops accepting invitations from organisations queuing up to ask him to talk at their functions. In the last 10 days, he has already attended three such public functions, a record that even the Prime Minister would find difficult to surpass.

Such public appearances and the speeches he delivered at these events give Dr Tan an unfair advantage over other prospective presidential candidates. They also make many wonder if the new normal in politics he spoke about is just a passing fantasy, and they leave a sour taste in the voter's mouth.

From a purely public relations point of view, his speeches and appearances are a smart way to show Dr Tan in different angles: As Mr Peranakan, Mr Economy and Mr Education. But politics is more than PR.

His presence at the Peranakan Association's 111th anniversary dinner on 9 July sparked a very relevant question in a posting in Javert's World: "Technically, he is jobless and his title is ex-Deputy Prime Minister, not even Emeritus. So how did he end up as a VIP of the Peranakan clan?"

And, let me add by asking: Why now?

Discussions on the economy, politics and education

Then came his lecture at the Singapore Chinese Chamber of Commerce six days later, on 15 July, where he gave his take on trends, risks and opportunites in the global economy, his favourite hobby horse. Even when he was Defence Minister, Dr Tan did not hesitate to give his views on Singapore's economic policy. But what caught the attention was his analysis of the result of GE 2011.

He positioned himself as an all-embracing avuncular elder statesman when he framed the post-GE scenario this way: A win-win-win outcome. A win for the PAP because the party won 81 of 87 seats; a win for the opposition, especially the Workers' Party, because it now has a base to build on its aspiration, credibility, influence "and possibly get even more votes in the next election"; and a win for Singapore as it takes political development here to a new level.

The next date in Dr Tan's crowded diary was 19 July when he again delivered a lecture, this time at the Singapore Management University, on the future of higher education. This one appeared even more strategic with the former executive director of the Government of Singapore Investment Corporation using the occasion to clarify online talk about his position on foreign students and the graduate mothers policy.

He has been accused of being the architect of the open-door policy on foreign students and has been questioned about his role in reversing the unpopular scheme to give graduate mothers an advantage in registering their children for Primary One.

On the first, he said he had always advocated a Singaporean-first, but not Singaporean-only, approach. But it was on the second point, that he tried to be evasive. The graduate mums policy was one of the hot-button issues in the 1984 election that brought the PAP's majority of votes cast to below 60 per cent. Dr Tan became Education Minister the next year and reversed the policy.

Extensive media coverage

Media reports have used this example to show that the man has an independent streak in him. The online world refused to buy this and asked whether he would have taken the same decision if not for the 1984 election setback and, more importantly, whether he had argued against the policy before its implementation.

His answer: "I see little benefit to say what might have happened. The point is, one looks at the issue when one has the authority to do something about it. And the important thing is, when you have the authority, you should exercise it wisely, and not in a hurried way, but after due deliberation."

Dr Tan's public pronouncements, though lacking in real news value, have been getting a lot of media exposure. The latest saw most of the newspapers giving the views of Dr Tan, the former chairman of the Singapore Press Holdings, Page One treatment, with *The Straits Times* going further by also reporting nearly every twist and turn of his quotes in a full page inside and using excerpts of his speech in the comment section.

Political battles are never fair. Some parties and personalities will always get more exposure. But the post of presidency, as the Prime Minister's Office said in a recent statement, is very different; it is an office that is dignified and the person who finally gets elected into that office must show that he won it after a fair and square contest. As long as man-made hurdles like this exist, let's not even start talking about the new normal in Singapore politics.

Reproduced with permission.

I paid a price for this commentary. Temasek Foundation did not renew my yearly contract to continue as Director of Asia Journalism Fellowship. I was the founder director of AJF since 2008. The Fellowship brings in about 15 journalists from Asia to stay in Singapore and explore a project of their choice.

5. TALKING ABOUT PRESS FREEDOM — WITH PN BALJI

by Cherian George

This article was first published in Freedomfromthepress.info on 14 November 2012.

At the Singapore Writers Festival on Saturday 10 November 2012, I spoke about my book Freedom From The Press *and Singapore's media system with PN Balji, former editor of* The New Paper *and* TODAY. *We also talked about* OB Markers, *the book by retired* Straits Times *group editor-in-chief Cheong Yip Seng, who was originally scheduled to speak but had to withdraw. Here is an edited transcript of our dialogue.*

Cherian:

I've been writing about the Singapore press and the need for press freedom for a long time, and I thought that it was probably time to try and bring everything together into some kind of systematic argument. The other reason for this book is the sense that I've had for a long time that Singapore could be and should be so much more than it is, in particular in terms of our intellectual and creative life. Many Singaporeans feel that we deserve more than we get in our national press.

The enigma has always been, how is it that newspapers that are not government owned – and it is a common myth that they are government owned, when the number one shareholder of SPH shares is Citibank followed by HSBC – have been subject to such enduring press controls. I emphasise *enduring*, because of course it doesn't take much brains to control anything for a day or a week or a month. But how is it possible for a group of men to have controlled the ideological space for decades with no sign of any erosion of its ability to control that space?

The PAP has been able to preserve its dominance – which may be fraying at the edges, but by and large preserve its dominance – with diminishing use of power. It is not difficult to preserve dominance if you are willing to ratchet up your abuses every year, applying more and more violence. The mystery in Singapore is that the dominance remains, but the violence has reduced. Which must mean that in place of violence – in place of locking up journalists under the ISA, in place of closing down newspapers – somehow they've managed to preserve their dominance in less violent ways. So what are these less violent ways? That's what my book tries to answer.

To cut a long story short, it boils down to the replacement of more overt external controls with more behind the scenes controls; economic inducements, for example, that promote a culture of self censorship. That's one of the answers. My book focuses largely on these more structural reasons; it goes into the laws as well as the non-legal controls.

One of my regrets about writing my book when I did was that, shortly after, my old boss Cheong Yip Seng came out with his insider account, *OB Markers*. To be very honest – and as a journalist trained to take myself out of the equation – if you can only afford to buy one book today, and you have a choice between *OB Markers* and *Freedom From The Press*, I would say buy *OB Markers* and not my book.

One reason is that I'm cheap – anyone who wants to talk to me about the press, I'll talk to you, just buy my coffee. Cheong Yip Seng is more elusive – so elusive that he didn't show up today! He's been an enigma for decades, even to those who worked with him closely. And he reveals things in his book that only he could reveal, because he was really at the frontline where decisions were taken. So, it's a goldmine for researchers.

I don't think there is anything in his book that contradicts my thesis; I see it more as a supplement. Whereas my book looks largely at more structural controls, he looks at the role of individuals in shaping the press. Primarily, Lee Kuan Yew, as well as editors like himself, selected ministers, chairmen of boards and so on. He does, in many cases, explain who did what and why.

So I thought a good place to start my conversation with Balji is to address this question – whether he believes that, given the structure that we have, the press system that we have, can individuals make a difference? Or, do we just give up?

Balji:
Cheong gives insights and inside stories that have never been revealed before. I was quite surprised at some of the details, and the details show the extent to which government interference was applied: even to nitty-gritty issues like stories on stamp collection, stories on selling of carpets, and the most surprising – I only realised it when I read the book – on the use of MSG. The person who intervened was Mr Lee Kuan Yew. So, it does give details that have never been revealed before.

The editors of Singapore, including me, have this unusual habit of taking their stories to the grave. Cheong has bucked the trend. But having said that, there are also a lot of stories that have not been told, which have been glossed over. So if anybody tells you this is a tell-all book, don't believe it. It's a tell-something book…

Cherian:
So there's still a gap waiting for Balji to fill before…

Balji:
… Before I go to the grave. Honestly, I have actually thought of writing a book, and I have actually sat down in front of the computer, written the title of the book (*Ink in the Blood*), written the chapter headlines…. And finally I've decided not to write it. If I write a book I want to say everything I know and that would have two problems. One is that a lot of these things happened in confidence, so I would have to break confidence, of good friends; and some of the discussions that happened were very secret discussions.

The second problem was that of a legal suit. I can go as far as to say that one chapter was titled "The day I said no to Lee Kuan Yew". There's no way I can report it. I've written the chapter, I've edited it, I've sent it to a lawyer friend, he says, no, you'll get into trouble. Anyway, I'll keep that chapter. After my death – and maybe after somebody else's death – this can be revealed.

But coming to Cherian's question. I left mainstream journalism in 2008. Since 2000 or just before that, I've always believed that individuals in media, especially the people in the senior levels, can make a difference. I've seen that happen, with Cheong Yip Seng's boss, Mr Peter Lim. He made a difference.

There are examples in Cheong's book, and one of them I remember vividly. During an election rally speech at Fullerton Square, Mr Lee Kuan Yew revealed the O-level results of Mr Chiam See Tong and the PAP candidate. He compared the two results. After that speech, Mr Peter Lim had a call to say, please reveal also his detailed results – what did he get for Maths, English, other subjects. Mr Peter Lim resisted, and resisted till the end, and never published those details.

Peter's argument was that it was not good for the media to publish this information, because people would wonder where we got the information, and it must be from government. And secondly, it's also not good for the government, because people would then say, look – to what extent the government goes to demolish opposition figures.

And it's not just Peter Lim. There are many others, too, who have tried to make a difference. But what I also notice is that, unfortunately, these people who tried to make a difference didn't last in the jobs.

And this comes to the other point that I want to talk about: the biggest sin in Singapore journalism is self-censorship. The title of Mr Cheong's book is *OB Markers*. First question is, who sets OB markers. Of course the government sets OB markers. But do OB markers remain? As society changes, as people change, OB markers have to change. But the government that sets the OB markers doesn't come and tell you that the OB markers have changed. So how do you know that the OB markers have changed? That can only come about if you test the waters.

That is, you think that is an OB marker, but you test it. No reaction comes, that means the OB marker on this issue has changed. If you don't test it, you will never know. And I get the sense that the media generally in Singapore is not active in testing the OB markers. In my view, the media and to a certain extent the country, would pay a big price for not doing this.

Cherian:

For those in the audience who are not from Singapore, I should explain this acronym: OB markers are out of bounds markers – basically limits of political acceptability. If you cross them, the punishment is not imprisonment or a fine but the loss of political capital. Which is why many bloggers don't care about OB markers, because they don't care about getting political capital – it's not relevant to them.

But anyone whose job depends in some way on the government, who needs to do business with the government – and this would include many civil society organisations – for them OB markers are relevant because you cannot afford to be blacklisted as an untrustworthy group and deny yourself access to funds, to influence among decision markers, and so on. So even NGOs are subject to OB markers, and certainly press people are, within the mainstream press, because their jobs are ultimately determined by boards of directors who are indirectly but essentially appointed by the government.

But I agree with you – and I am probably guilty of it myself – we don't do enough to test those OB markers. Testing the OB markers requires, I think, quite a clinical calculation and ultimately depends on your own values. If the worst they can do to you is maybe impose a glass ceiling on your promotion and you lose the chance to be promoted to a senior position, you calculate and ask yourself, do you want that in the first place.

So what if you are looked at with a certain amount of distrust, does that mean you can't put food on the table? Singapore is not that bad, unlike some extremely dictatorial regimes where, if you are blacklisted, it may end your life or end your means of making a living. Here, you can cross OB markers and still put food on the table; it's just that you have to moderate your ambitions career-wise.

Balji:
Or you can leave the profession.

Cherian:
But it is very human to just choose the comfortable route where you don't have to pay the price of losing political capital.

And that leads me to a second thing I wanted to discuss with you. Since writing my book – and I notice that Cheong got the same reaction – when we present some of these facts of government intervention, and government control, it is of course uncomfortable for those currently in the system, whether it's civil servants, ministers or journalists. And I've noticed one defence mechanism– to say that, well, these books are about the past; things are better now; the knuckleduster era is over, it is much easier to say things, the government is much more accommodating of alternative views.

I have my doubts about that, whether things are really much better now than before. But I'd love to hear your views, Balji.

Balji:
I don't have doubts – it's a fact. In my experience, when Mr Lee Kuan Yew was at his rogue best, there were journalists who actually stood up to some of that, and of course to some extent paid the price. Now, there's a bit more openness, and I would have expected for the testing

of waters to be a bit more robust. And I am quite surprised and even shocked that it actually doesn't happen as much as it should. And this is the time to test it. The mainstream media seems to have gone even more into a shell.

Cherian:
Of course, the easy answer to that is that journalists are more lazy now. But I'm very suspicious of these sorts of individual-level explanations. I would rather look for structural explanations before I blame individuals, and I think one structural explanation could be that precisely because the internet has emerged as a platform on which the government gets attacked every day, the government is guarding its control of mainstream media even more jealously.

There are really two routes that the government could go. One is to say, look, Singapore is changing very fast; the electorate is becoming more demanding; the internet is becoming more vociferous; so the mainstream media better change quickly, otherwise they will lose all credibility and be of no service to us either. I think many of us feel that that is a rational course of action.

But there's another policy response which is that, precisely because things are changing so fast, we'd better hold on to the centre. And that centre, ideologically, is the mainstream media; so we'd better supervise it as strictly as ever before because we can't trust anything else. Everything else is spinning out of control, but we can continue to control the media.

The other reason is that it's a moving target. Yes, it is true that things could be said in the *Straits Times* today that couldn't be said five or ten years ago. For example, we are much more open now about sexual politics and the mere existence of gays. We are much more open now about criticising unpopular government policies. So in absolute terms, of course there is an opening up. But public expectations have also moved.

The way the opposition is getting coverage now would have absolutely delighted J B Jeyaretnam 20 years ago, because he did not get that kind of mileage in the press. But expectations have also risen.

And this is not an accident. The system is designed to ensure that the mainstream press is always slightly behind the curve. It is never an avant garde institution. The whole reason for the press controls is to ensure that the mainstream press is not an unadulterated reflection of popular opinion, and certainly not a vehicle for the most progressive forces in society. The whole intention is to ensure that the mainstream press is largely a centrist, conservative institution. There's no way we can expect the press to play a leading intellectual role until we look at those press controls.

Balji:

I think it's also natural that once you control something as powerful as media, to give that control up, it goes against nature.

What I still don't get is, if the mainstream media continues to be behind the curve, who is the biggest loser? The biggest loser is the government, because the eyeballs will move away from mainstream media. It's already moving. The Straits Times circulation is dipping. I still remember when Cheong Yip Seng was editor in chief, he would boast we don't have to worry about circulation as long as there is a housing building programme. Every time there is a new block of HDB flats, our circulation will go up. How things have changed. Now the *Straits Times* even offers massage chairs in a contest if you become a subscriber.

And there is no other platform for the government to get across its messages. My guess is that they don't think they have reached the danger zone yet.

Audience member:

As an outsider I've been quite surprised to see issues like xenophobia, HIV and gays so openly spoken about. Why is it so important to talk about politics – isn't it enough to talk about social and health related issues? Some would argue that if you open the social space – that's what's needed now?

Cherian:
Isn't it OK, if you have this flowering in different social sectors, for your politics to be controlled? I think at some point all social policies touch on politics. You can pursue certain causes, whether it's animal rights or workers rights or gay rights up to a point; beyond a certain point, it does threaten government dominance in some way.

Pursuing animal rights at some point becomes a threat to the economic viability of the Singapore Zoo; so at some point it stops being a soft and fuzzy issue and affects what the government considers to be the bottom line. So I don't think it's possible to compartmentalise those issues.

Audience member:
Perhaps the majority of people may have made a Faustian pact, that as long as things are OK, we are not concerned about press freedom. As the left wing theorist Gramsci said, there is a cultural superstructure which governs all of us; after a while, we internalise all these things and therefore it becomes naturalised, and we don't see anymore that we have no press freedom. As long as there is no other issue on which this issue of press freedom can ride on, it will never become a major issue, and therefore the government can calibrate and doesn't have to use force. Would you agree that it really doesn't matter to most people?

Cherian:
I will keep my answer short – Yes.

Balji:

I don't really agree, Cherian. Since I left my fulltime job four years ago, I have had this great opportunity to meet all kinds of people. If you use the term press freedom, then it becomes very narrow; but if you talk in general terms, in which press freedom is just one aspect of a gamut of issues, then I think it's not just the upper crust that talk about the issues; a lot of people are very upset about the things they think happen in Singapore. So I am not that convinced that it is only a small group of people.

Cherian:

I'm going to do a Mitt Romney and say yes to you, too. I absolutely see where Balji is coming from. If you ask the average Singaporean, whoever that is, do you agree we should have more press freedom and human rights, they will say: I don't know, we are an Asian society, etc.. It kind of activates certain things we have been brought up to believe. But, if you ask: if there is a disagreement between people like you and the government, do you think newspapers and journalists should side with you or with the government? – I think most ordinary people will say, oh, side with us. What is that, if not press freedom? So I think often it's the way the question is asked.

Reproduced with permission.

I enjoyed this conversation very much. Seven years later, the issues we talked about remain very real.

6. A LEGACY IN THE MAKING

Singapore's Lee marks 10 years as PM, amid debate over the city-state's future direction

by PN Balji

This article was first published in *The Edge Review*, Malaysia, in September 2014.

It has been 10 years since Lee Hsien Loong became prime minister of Singapore, yet his style and achievements are hard to put a finger on, as Singapore grapples with a maturing economy, a population mix that throws up questions about national identity and inequality and a citizenry that has suddenly been let loose by a vibrant and raucous online world.

There was no mistake about what founding Prime Minister Lee Kuan Yew and his successor, Goh Chok Tong, stood for very early in their leadership years. Pushed to the wall by racial and ethnic riots, separation from the Federation of Malaya, and the withdrawal of British troops, the best and worst of LKY came out. He was bent on building an economic miracle, even if it meant he had to put his opponents behind bars.

After 31 years of LKY's reign, which saw Singapore punching above its weight as a regional economic powerhouse but receiving international ridicule for its human rights record, Goh identified a sweet spot to position his prime ministership as one that would make the country a caring one. Although there were instances that made him take a hard line, generally his reign was a gentler and kinder one.

But Singapore's third prime minister, Lee Hsien Loong, is still struggling to make a mark for himself. In short, he is suffering from an identity crisis. Three factors have made his job a very tough one.

A huge hurdle is his cabinet, the weakest when compared with those of his predecessors. LKY was blessed to have path-breakers such his deputy, Goh Keng Swee, who should actually be remembered as the real architect of Singapore. His credentials were impressive and his contributions were groundbreaking, with many of the country's present institutions still bearing the trademark of that loyal lieutenant.

Goh started the army, transformed a wasteland in Jurong into one giant industrial estate, set up the Monetary Authority of Singapore and the Economic Development Board and played an influential role in the formation of the Singapore Zoo and Singapore Symphony Orchestra.

The brains behind the second prime minister's Cabinet was none other than Lee Hsien Loong, the deputy who masterminded Singapore's escape from the recession of 1985. A former civil servant who had dealings with him said: "Once I sent Lee Hsien Loong a position paper; within 30 ministers, I got a response with questions and comments that revealed his grasp of details and his acute understanding of world affairs."

Now that Lee is prime minister, that kind of Cabinet talent is missing.

Second, he and his team have been dealt the cruellest card in the form of a political game-changer called the Internet. For a leadership brought up on a command-and-control culture, the influence of the online world was something with which it was unable to deal. The result was a humiliating election result that took the ruling party's share of popular vote to a historic low of 60.1 per cent three years ago – a per cent that would be the envy of ruling parties in most other countries, but which signaled an erosion of public support in Singapore's traditionally monolithic political culture.

LKY and Goh had it much easier with just one voice – that of His Majesty, LKY – drowning out every other voice in town.

Third, and this is a little speculative, Lee Hsien Loong must have found it very difficult to move out of the shadow of his father, the first and founding prime minister, and act decisively when he needed to. Act tough, and the accusation that he is his father's boy would prevail.

Early into his leadership eight years ago and during the heat of a general election, the prime minister snapped: I will have to spend my time fixing the opposition if they win too many seats.

That had his father's brutal temperament and strong language written all over it. The prime minister understood the folly of his statement and apologised immediately.

In fact, it is his lack of decisiveness – especially against his ruling team – that has highlighted a major part of his leadership years. His 10-year reign has seen him moving from one crisis to another, with the prime minister being put on the backfoot and displaying a palpable reluctance to call a spade a spade.

Among the notable developments on his watch: the escape of terrorist Mas Selamat from a maximum security prison, the first labour strike in 26 years, the first riot in 40 years, sex and corruption scandals involving two top civil servants and finally the major strategic error of bringing too many foreigners into the country when the infrastructure was not there to handle the crush.

Even today, it is a mystery why such a forward-looking government that displays its scenario-planning skills on its sleeves with great pride never saw this storm coming. Lee Hsien Loong and his government are still paying the price for that misstep. The housing and transport building programmes, which kicked in soon after the disastrous 2011 general election results, will take a while to show results.

But for those who closely examine Lee's roller coaster ride, it may well be that his lasting legacy will be more forgiving than contemporary judgements of him, because he has taken steps to steer Singapore toward a series of policies that will represent a break from the city-state's past. For these, he may well be remembered for having succeeded, precisely because he departed from the legacies of his father and further entrenched his predecessor's move to make Singapore a more caring society

Lee's biggest achievement has been in helping to launch a peaceful and beneficial relationship with Singapore's closest neighbour, Malaysia. The personal warmth established with Prime Minister Najib Abdul Razak has taken the sting out of 50 years of acrimonious relations with Singapore's closest neighbour. The railway land deal, which eluded both his predecessors, was signed and delivered under Lee Hsien Loong's leadership.

He has also pushed hard to level the playing field for the slow learners by establishing special schools for them and taking a personal interest in showcasing industrial training colleges that cater for those who fall through the examination cracks.

Signs are also emerging that the prime minister will plant his personal flag on a couple of welfare policies. Universal insurance coverage and a generous health package for the pioneer generation are kicking in, with the prime minister taking a personal interest to make sure that schemes are not hijacked by critics waiting to scuttle his plans.

He is at the half-way mark of his prime ministership and the chances are that his move to shift Singapore away from a nothing-is-for-free country to one that is prepared to take some bold steps towards semi-welfarism will succeed. Until then, the identity crisis will continue to haunt a prime minister who came to power after a charmed entry into politics 30 years ago.

Reproduced with permission.

This was a look at Lee Hsien Loong's ten years as PM. I made the point that his Cabinet did not have the kind of talent that the two PMs before him had.

7. BOLD CHANGES TO LKY'S SINGAPORE

by PN Balji

This article was first published in *The Edge Review*, Malaysia, in September 2014.

Lee Kuan Yew marked his 9st birthday on Tuesday in a Singapore that is looking very different from the one he moulded both physically and ideologically. He makes occasional visits to the new downtown created in the Marina Bay area, visiting superstructures such as the Gardens by the Bay, the Barrage and the casino to soak in the new Singapore.

But there is another Singapore that might not please the founding father so much, as he sees the ruling party he founded by manipulating and outsmarting the British colonialists, communists and rivals edging away from his ideals and ideologies.

It is a Singapore that his son, Prime Minister Lee Hsien Loong, is forced to shape as he struggles to respond to a population that wants more freedom, a bigger share of the pie that the government has baked practically from scratch, and an escape from the pressure-cooker life in a crowded and expensive city. Not to mention, he has to reverse the downward trend in votes for the ruling party, which has dropped to a historic low of 60.1 per cent under his rule.

The younger Lee has promised older Singaporeans that they can live out their august years in "peace of mind" with his socialist-leaning policies that will partially subsidise their health care costs. During the LKY era, "subsidy" was a dirty word and anyone who dared utter it would have received a tongue lashing and possible blacklisting.

For these Singaporeans, it is not just health and money that matter. The government seems to ignore – at least publicly – that growing old gracefully in a crowded and compact city is nearly impossible.

I am hitting 66 and living in a city state with no hinterland to escape to can be downright depressing. Driving in crowded and toll-charging roads sends your blood pressure up and leaves a deep hole in a shrinking pocket. Weekends are a nightmare. I avoid cinemas and shopping centres like the plague, because they are full of people who make you feel like a stranger at best and a misfit at worst.

How to have "peace of mind" like this?

Then there is the audacious – even outrageous – initiative to turn the LKY team's obsession with academic degrees on its head. The prime minister wants Singaporeans "not to go on a paper chase for qualifications or degrees, especially if they are not relevant."

Like nearly everything else in Singapore, committees have been formed to make this happen. One has come out with ideas on how polytechnic students can get their diploma, get a job and further their studies at the same time. Another committee, chaired by deputy prime minister Tharman Shanmugaratnam, is looking at how to get employers' support and social recognition for those who move up the ladder because of their skills, not just their degrees.

All this flies in the face of government policies that have increased the number of universities from three to six in the last five years, with bosses and parents encouraging the paper chase.

Applications to universities go up in number every year, and those who don't make it go overseas or to private schools.

The government is the biggest culprit in encouraging the chase for the holy grail of a degree, with politicians and civil servants being head-hunted based on their paper qualifications.

There was even a time, in 1984, when LKY angered so many Singaporeans with his theory that graduate women should get married and have children because their offspring will turn out to be smarter than those born to non-graduates.

He went to the extent of giving children of such graduate wives priority in getting into schools of their choice, which angered a newspaper reader so much that she called the group promoting the policy "storm troopers."

How will the prime minister be able to change course on a culture of elitism so ingrained in bosses, workers, youth and parents?

How will the prime minister be able to bring about "peace of mind" to an ageing population struggling to lead peaceful lives in a country that wants to remain youthful forever?

Lee Hsien Loong has a fight on his hands.

Reproduced with permission.

Another column on PM Lee Hsien Loong which talked about how he was trying to move out of his father's shadow to realise a new Singapore.

8. THE ENDURING MIDDLE EASTERN MEXICANS

by PN Balji

This article was first published in *The Edge Review*, Malaysia, in September 2014.

One of the marvels of international diplomacy is how Israel and Singapore used subterfuge and deception to conduct a military relationship that, despite 49 years of closeness, is still shrouded in mystery.

Bits and pieces of the dark story have made it into the public space, with some of the most authoritative ones appearing in one of the volumes of Lee Kuan Yew's autobiography. Lee masterfully managed the relationship by taking care of nearly every detail to make sure that everything fit perfectly into a neat little puzzle.

Even the date of the arrival of Israeli advisers to help set up the backbone of Singapore's military was chosen to defy suspicion. The first group of six officers and their families slipped into Singapore on Christmas Eve in 1965, four months after Singapore's independence, and thus began a relationship that has made Singapore an envied and feared military force in this part of the world, just as Israel is in the Middle East.

"To disguise their presence, we called them Mexicans. They looked swarthy enough," said LKY in the first volume of his autobiography, *From Third World to First: The Singapore Story 1965–2000*.

Explaining the need for secrecy, he wrote: "We had to ensure, as far as possible, that the arrival of the Israelis will not become public knowledge in order not to arouse opposition among the Malay Muslims who live in Malaysia and Singapore."

Other details of the relationship were reported in an Israeli newspaper, *Haaretz*, 10 years ago. It had interviews with the Israeli officers who played important roles in the formative years. They talked about how Singapore had used India and Egypt essentially as a ruse to make the world believe that Israel was not on the radar screen.

LKY told the Israelis that he had actually asked India and Egypt for help in building up the city-state's armed forces. *Haaertz* speculated that Singapore had all along wanted Israeli involvement and was quite sure that India and Egypt would decline their offer for assistance. And it was to show the world that Israel was not its first choice.

A testing time appeared in 1967, when Israel was engaged in the Yom Kippur War. LKY writes: "We were relieved that the Israelis were not defeated or our forces would have lost confidence."

Although the Israeli presence was kept a secret, Singapore was wily enough to reveal its strength when the need arose. In the 1969 National Day parade, the country showcased 30 tanks it had just bought from Israel. And Malaysia's defence minister was one of the guests present.

"It had a dramatic effect," writes LKY. Because Malaysia at that time had no tanks, it was a signal to Singapore's larger neighbour to think twice before launching any attack against Singapore.

It was like a partnership made in heaven. Both countries are small, surrounded by Muslim neighbours and their governments need to create a siege mentality in order to make their citizens take security seriously. Israel needed to be recognised and respected for its military might. Singapore fitted the bill.

From day one, the Israelis wanted to make sure this was an enduring relationship and that they were not fly-by-night operators. In a revealing interview with *Haaertz*, one Israeli general said he told his people: "When you recommend items to procure, use the purest professional military judgment."

This kind of straight talk and professional judgement was evident when now retired Singaporean banker Eric Tan wanted some advice on whether he should join the air force or go and take up a degree course in university.

Tan told *The Edge Review*: "The Israeli officer was clear and concise. He told me to go and do the degree."

In the 49 years of this controversial and mysterious relationship, there was only one time when it erupted into a major diplomatic fight. Malaysia and Indonesia were up in arms when Singapore invited then Israeli President Chaim Herzog to visit Singapore. But the incident blew over after LKY admitted it was wrong to invite Herzog, but insisted that once the deed was done, there was no way Singapore was going to back out.

As the relationship morphed into collaboration among the two in their respective defence industries, Israel's recent actions in Gaza against Hamas has put the Singapore government in a spot with its own Malay citizens. The Internet has been abuzz with Israel's bloodletting, leaving Singapore's leaders to try to walk a fine line between criticising Israel and calling for a ceasefire.

That kind of balancing act might not just work in the Internet world.

Reproduced with permission.

Singapore's relationship with Israel has been contentious and mysterious. As I dug into the research, I was surprised by how both countries used subterfuge and deception to keep their military relationship under cover.

9. BILAHARI KAUSIKAN, SINGAPORE'S UNDIPLOMATIC DIPLOMAT

by PN Balji

This article was first published in Yahoo News on 2 November 2015.

I like him, I like him not. I have listened to some of his speeches, sat in on some of his briefings and followed his Facebook posts closely.

Ambassador at large Bilahari Kausikan impresses with his intellect, witty rejoinders and say-it-as-it-is statements. He can go berserk when attacking critics of Singapore. In a recent Facebook post, he said a freelancer was writing critical articles about Singapore for a Malaysian website because of the money she can make out of it.

And just the other day, Kausikan had this smart-ass post on Han Hui Hui, who is facing charges of causing public nuisance during a protest rally at Hong Lim Park: "I think HHH … should plead not guilty for reasons of insanity."

Nothing seems to scare him, even making unsavoury statements about politics and politicians of other countries. Earlier this month, he waded into Malaysian politics when he wrote that Chinese Malaysians were being delusional if they think the principle of Malay dominance can be changed. "Malay dominance will be defended by any means," he thundered. Malaysian opposition politician Tony Pua hit back calling Singapore the mercenary prick of South-east Asia.

He brings back images of an era when Lee Kuan Yew reigned supreme with his undiplomatic attacks on countries like Malaysia, Australia, India. Kausikan, as the permanent secretary in the Ministry of Foreign Affairs, was at the centre of it all when LKY and Mahathir Mohamad were taking relations between the two countries to the edge of the cliff.

It is the school of LKY that Kausikan graduated from and you can see heavy doses of what he has learnt in his responses. Recently, he got into a verbal fight with France and its European allies when he accused Paris of being "hobbled by its own absolutist beliefs" on human rights. Two European ambassadors responded but Kausikan wanted to have the last word.

"Why throw the weight of the state against discrimination against one religion or group, while acquiescing in the systematic vilification of another religion, Islam, in the name of freedom of speech?" he asked in a pointed reference to the satirical Charlie Hebdo magazine.

There are enough examples like these to show how undiplomatic this diplomat has become. No one in government seems to have pulled him back and so far his messy musings don't seem to have affected Singapore's relations with other countries.

Maybe, they have come to terms with a man they consider to be a loose cannon who doesn't have policy-making powers. It might also be possible that Singapore considers such a character useful to tell the world what Singapore really feels about world affairs but does not articulate publicly.

Kausikan is a breath of fresh air in the civil service where officers hardly say a word in public for fear of reprisals from their bosses. Kausikan is an open book; his views, whether you like them or not, are there for readers to agree with or dispute. And I am sure he will be ready to respond robustly against his detractors.

A good measure of the man is available in an interview he gave to a Public Service Division publication, Challenge. "I say what I think. I'm me, I can't be anything but me," he said.

For all his candour, he remains rather cagey when it comes to commenting on Singapore's policy missteps. He has been silent on how

Singapore got into a mess when the public housing policy backfired under Mah Bow Tan or when the exuberant immigration policy caused a transport nightmare for the government.

History will salute him if he does that.

Reproduced with permission.

I was expecting a thunderous response. But Bilahari decided otherwise. He said in his FB post: Unlike most online commentators, I write only on matters where I have some expertise in and which may be of use to my compatriots. I see no reason to write just to stir controversy which is what Mr Balji wants me to do.

10. CONFESSIONS OF A GRANDFATHER
Breaking the Arrian Code

by PN Balji
This article was first published in The Independent on 27 February 2016.

Finally, I have broken the Arrian code. Seven years of dealing with a boisterous, fearless, restless and rebellious boy, this grandfather is slowly beginning to find the pieces of the magic formula on how to deal with him.

There were moments when I nearly gave up. Thank goodness I didn't. Now I see only a doting older brother, a caring son and a loving grandson. The other traits … well, they don't matter.

I used to see only the outside of Arrian. He is impatient with his answers – that is, if he does answer your questions at all – and occasionally uses words that I don't want to repeat here. Getting him to focus on something is near impossible. And trying to start a conversation with him can make my blood pressure go up.

Me: How was school?

Arrian: Good.

Me: How was your Malay spelling test?

Arrian: Fail.

When I look at his exercise book, it shows a perfect score. Those were frustrating times.

For my own peace of mind and fearing that the tension in the relationship will sour, I decided to change tact. I decided to focus only on his positive factors. His mind works in strange ways. I have watched him build, bit by bit, his model airport at home with patience and diligence.

I have seen the airport grow from just a handful of planes to include the control tower, aerobridges, a hangar, ambulances, police cars and the various terminal buildings. I make it a point to talk to him about his airport.

I take him to Changi and Seletar airports, give him clippings of newspaper stories of planes and narrate my own experiences in airports I have visited. He is obsessed with the MH370 flight that disappeared on its way from KL to Beijing two years ago and I tap into that to talk about other air mishaps.

And last Sunday, I took Arrian to the air show. I asked him if he knew how to get to the venue by train.

"Take the train to Bishan, change at Paya Lebar, change again at Tanah Merah to reach the Expo station."

He goes to great lengths to spend time on projects he initiates. Classroom settings put him off. I remember taking him to an aerospace adventure club during the year-end holidays. As we we were entering the club at Seletar, he asked me: "Is it going to be like in a class room?" It was clear that he didn't want to go back to a school setting during his holidays.

Some of his questions have baffled me. When told that the collective noun for fishes is school, he shot back: "How come they are not wearing uniforms?" Immediately came his own answer: "Because the uniforms will get wet."

The way he takes over the responsibility of talking to his younger brother is heart-warming. Once, their father was trying to talk to his three-year-old at night because Roman had smuggled some sweets in his pocket and wanted to eat them.

This is what his father said in a family Whatsapp group chat: "Roman had wanted to eat sweets before his bedtime. I told him to hand them over. Arrian swiftly intervened, knelt down to his brother's eye level and explained to him that eating sweets now will give him indigestion (his word)."

When his father told him to give a speech on my birthday in December, he sprung up immediately and gave a short speech that surprised all present. He ended by looking at me and saying: "Thank you for teaching me Malay."

The story behind these stories is that bringing up children is a full-time job that needs skill, creativity, passion, strategies, tactics, love, patience ...

You do it because you want to, not because you have to. Maids, teachers, relatives are just an adjunct. They help you to take care of the extras. You provide the core.

My attitude towards Arrian changed after I saw how he took an instant liking to his boxing coach. I told coach Bala some of the characteristics of the boy. Coach Bala's strategy was an eye-opener. He introduced Arrian to the rest of his students with these words: "This is Arrian. Look at him, his body, the way he walks and talks. He will make a great boxer. He is my little hero."

Arrian melted in front of him.

Thank you, coach. You have helped a grandfather understand his grandson better.

Reproduced with permission.

Arrian is now 11 years and is growing up to be a confident and articulate boy. I am glad his parents transferred him out of a well-known Singapore school to an international school.

ABOUT THE AUTHOR

PN Balji is a veteran journalist with more than 40 years' experience in Singapore journalism and has worked in five newspapers, three of them as editor. His experience spans print, broadcast and digital journalism. He is one of Singapore's most well-known media personalities and has provided communications advisory services to both public and private sector organisations in Singapore, including government ministries, statutory boards and tertiary institutions.